I0471922

Congressional Research Service

U.S. Energy: Overview and Key Statistics

Carl E. Behrens
Specialist in Energy Policy

Carol Glover
Information Research Specialist

April 11, 2012

Congressional Research Service

7-5700

www.crs.gov

R40187

CRS Report for Congress
Prepared for Members and Committees of Congress

Summary

Energy supplies and prices are major economic factors in the United States, and energy markets are volatile and unpredictable. Thus, energy policy has been a recurring issue for Congress since the first major crisis in the 1970s. As an aid in policy making, this report presents a current and historical view of the supply and consumption of various forms of energy.

The historical trends show petroleum as the major source of energy, rising from about 38% in 1950 to 45% in 1975, then declining to about 40% in response to the energy crisis of the 1970s. Significantly, the transportation sector continues to be almost completely dependent on petroleum, mostly gasoline. The importance of this dependence on the volatile world oil market was revealed over the past five years as perceptions of impending inability of the industry to meet increasing world demand led to three years of steady increases in the prices of oil and gasoline. With the downturn in the world economy and a consequent decline in consumption, prices collapsed, but then recovered to a much higher level than in the 1990s. With the crisis in Libya in the Spring of 2011, oil and gasoline prices began again to approach their former peak levels. By 2012, Libyan production had recovered, but a new crisis involving Iran further threatened supply.

Natural gas followed a long-term pattern of U.S. consumption similar to that of oil, at a lower level. Its share of total energy increased from about 17% in 1950 to more than 30% in 1970, then declined to about 20%. Natural gas markets are very much more regional than the petroleum market, in which events in one part of the world tend to influence consumption and prices everywhere. Recent development of large deposits of shale gas in the United States have increased the outlook for U.S. natural gas supply and consumption in the near future. Consumption of coal in 1950 was 35% of the total, almost equal to oil, but it declined to about 20% a decade later and has remained at about that proportion since then. Coal currently is used almost exclusively for electric power generation, and its contribution to increased production of carbon dioxide has made its use controversial in light of concerns about global climate change.

Nuclear power started coming online in significant amounts in the late 1960s. By 1975, in the midst of the oil crisis, it was supplying 9% of total electricity generation. However, increases in capital costs, construction delays, and public opposition to nuclear power following the Three Mile Island accident in 1979 curtailed expansion of the technology, and many construction projects were cancelled. Continuation of some construction increased the nuclear share of generation to 20% in 1990, where it remains currently. Licenses for a number of new nuclear units have been in the works for several years, and preliminary construction for a few units has begun, but the economic downturn has discouraged action on new construction. The accident at Japan's Fukushima station following the March 2011 earthquake and tsunami raised further questions about future construction of nuclear powerplants.

Construction of major hydroelectric projects has also essentially ceased, and hydropower's share of electricity generation has gradually declined, from 30% in 1950 to 15% in 1975 and less than 10% in 2000. However, hydropower remains highly important on a regional basis.

Renewable energy sources (except hydropower) continue to offer more potential than actual energy production, although fuel ethanol has become a significant factor in transportation fuel. Wind power has recently grown rapidly, although it still contributes only a small share of total electricity generation. Conservation and energy efficiency have shown significant gains over the past three decades and offer potential to relieve some of the dependence on oil imports.

Contents

Figures

Tables

Contacts

Introduction

Tracking changes in energy activity is complicated by variations in different energy markets. These markets, for the most part, operate independently, although events in one may influence trends in another. For instance, oil price movement can affect the price of natural gas, which then plays a significant role in the price of electricity. Since aggregate indicators of total energy production and consumption do not adequately reflect these complexities, this compendium focuses on the details of individual energy sectors. Primary among these are oil, particularly gasoline for transportation, and electricity generation and consumption. Natural gas is also an important energy source, for home heating as well as in industry and electricity generation. Coal is used almost entirely for electricity generation, nuclear and hydropower completely so.[1]

Renewable sources (except hydropower) continue to offer more potential than actual energy production, although fuel ethanol has become a significant factor in transportation fuel. Wind power also has recently grown rapidly, although it still contributes only a small share of total electricity generation. Conservation and energy efficiency have shown significant gains over the past three decades, and offer encouraging potential to relieve some of the dependence on imports that has caused economic difficulties in the past as well as the present.

To give a general view of energy consumption trends, **Table 1** shows consumption by economic sector—residential, commercial, transportation, and industry—from 1950 to the present. To supplement this overview, some of the trends are highlighted in **Figure 1** and **Figure 2**.

In viewing these figures, a note on units of energy may be helpful. Each source has its own unit of energy. Oil consumption, for instance, is measured in million barrels per day (mbd),[2] coal in million tons per year, natural gas in trillion cubic feet (tcf) per year. To aggregate various types of energy in a single table, a common measure, British Thermal Unit (Btu), is often used. In **Table 1**, energy consumption by sector is given in units of quadrillion Btus per year, or "quads," while per capita consumption is given in million Btus (MMBtu) per year. One quad corresponds roughly to one tcf of natural gas, or approximately 50 million tons of coal. One million barrels per day of oil is approximately 2 quads per year. One million Btus is equivalent to approximately 293 kilowatt-hours (Kwh) of electricity. Electric power generating capacity is expressed in terms of kilowatts (Kw), megawatts (Mw, equals 1,000 Kw) or gigawatts (Gw, equals 1,000 Mw). Gas-fired plants are typically about 250 Mw, coal-fired plants usually more than 500 Mw, and large nuclear powerplants are typically about 1.2 Gw in capacity.

Table 1 shows that total U.S. energy consumption almost tripled since 1950, with the industrial sector, the heaviest energy user, growing at the slowest rate. The growth in energy consumption per capita (i.e., per person) over the same period was about 50%. As **Figure 1** illustrates, much of the growth in per capita energy consumption took place before 1970.

---

[1] This report focuses on current and historical consumption and production of energy. For a description of the resource base from which energy is supplied, see CRS Report R40872, *U.S. Fossil Fuel Resources: Terminology, Reporting, and Summary*, by Carl E. Behrens, Michael Ratner, and Carol Glover.

[2] Further complications can result from the fact that not all sources use the same abbreviations for the various units. The Energy Information Administration (EIA), for example, abbreviates "million barrels per day" as "MMbbl/d" rather than "mbd." For a list of EIA's abbreviation forms for energy terms, see http://www.eia.doe.gov/neic/a-z/a-z_abbrev/a-z_abbrev.html.

Table 1 does not list the consumption of energy by the electricity sector separately because it is both a producer and a consumer of energy. For the residential, commercial, industrial, and transportation sectors, the consumption figures given are the sum of the resources (such as oil and gas) that are directly consumed plus the total energy used to produce the electricity each sector consumes—that is, both the energy value of the kilowatt-hours consumed and the energy lost in generating that electricity. As **Figure 2** demonstrates, a major trend during the period was the electrification of the residential and commercial sectors and, to a lesser extent, industry. By 2010, electricity (including the energy lost in generating it) represented about 70% of residential energy consumption, about 80% of commercial energy consumption, and about a third of industrial energy consumption.[3]

Table 1. U.S. Energy Consumption, 1950-2010

	Energy Consumption by Sector (Quadrillion Btu)					Population (millions)	Consumption Per Capita (Million Btu)		
	Resid.	Comm.	Indust.	Trans.	Total		Total	Resid.	Trans.
1950	6.0	3.9	16.2	8.5	34.6	152.3	227.3	39.3	55.8
1955	7.3	3.9	19.5	9.6	40.2	165.9	242.3	43.9	57.6
1960	9.0	4.6	20.8	10.6	45.1	180.7	249.5	50.0	58.6
1965	10.6	5.8	25.1	12.4	54.0	194.3	278.0	54.8	64.0
1970	13.8	8.3	29.6	16.1	67.8	205.1	330.8	67.1	78.5
1975	14.8	9.5	29.4	18.2	72.0	216.0	333.2	68.6	84.5
1980	15.8	10.6	32.0	19.7	78.1	227.2	343.6	69.3	86.7
1985	16.0	11.5	28.8	20.1	76.4	237.9	321.1	67.4	84.4
1990	16.9	13.3	31.8	22.4	84.5	249.6	338.5	67.9	89.8
1995	18.5	14.7	34.0	23.8	91.0	266.3	341.9	69.5	89.6
2000	20.4	17.2	34.7	26.5	98.8	282.2	350.2	72.4	94.1
2005	21.6	17.9	32.4	28.4	100.3	295.6	339.2	73.2	95.9
2006	20.7	17.7	32.4	28.8	99.6	298.4	333.8	69.4	96.6
2007	21.6	18.3	32.4	29.1	101.4	301.4	336.3	71.6	96.6
2008	21.6	18.4	31.3	28.0	99.3	304.2	326.4	71.0	92.1
2009	21.1	17.9	28.5	27.0	94.5	306.7	308.1	68.7	88.0
2010P	22.2	18.2	30.1	27.5	98.0	309.1	317.1	71.7	89.0

Source: Energy Information Administration (EIA), *Annual Energy Review 2010*, Tables 2.1a and D1. Per capita data calculated by CRS.

Notes: Data for 2010 are preliminary.

---

[3] In calculating these percentages, "electric energy consumption" includes both the energy value of the kilowatt-hours consumed and the energy lost in generating that electricity.

Figure 1. Per Capita Energy Consumption in Transportation and Residential Sectors, 1950-2010

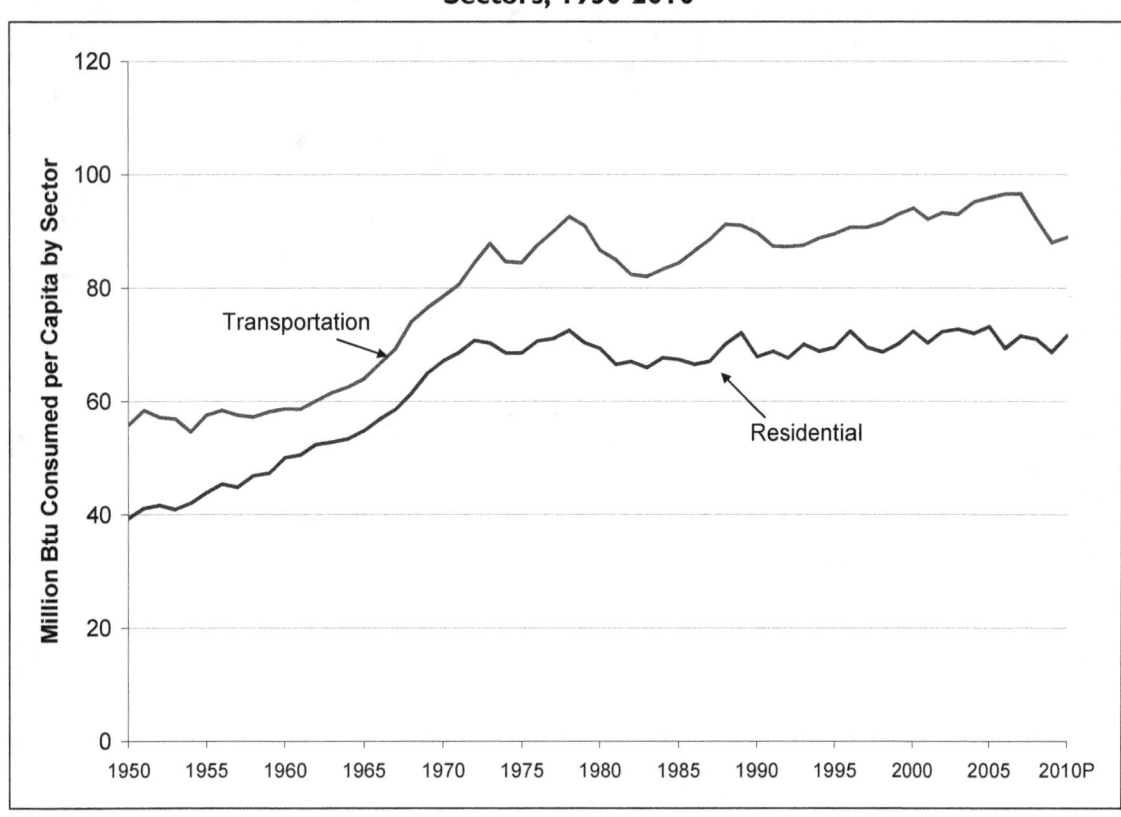

Source: Energy Information Administration (EIA), *Annual Energy Review 2010*, Tables 2.1a and D1. Per capita data calculated by CRS.

Notes: Data for 2010 are preliminary.

Figure 2. Electricity Intensity: Commercial, Residential, and Industrial Sectors, 1950-2010

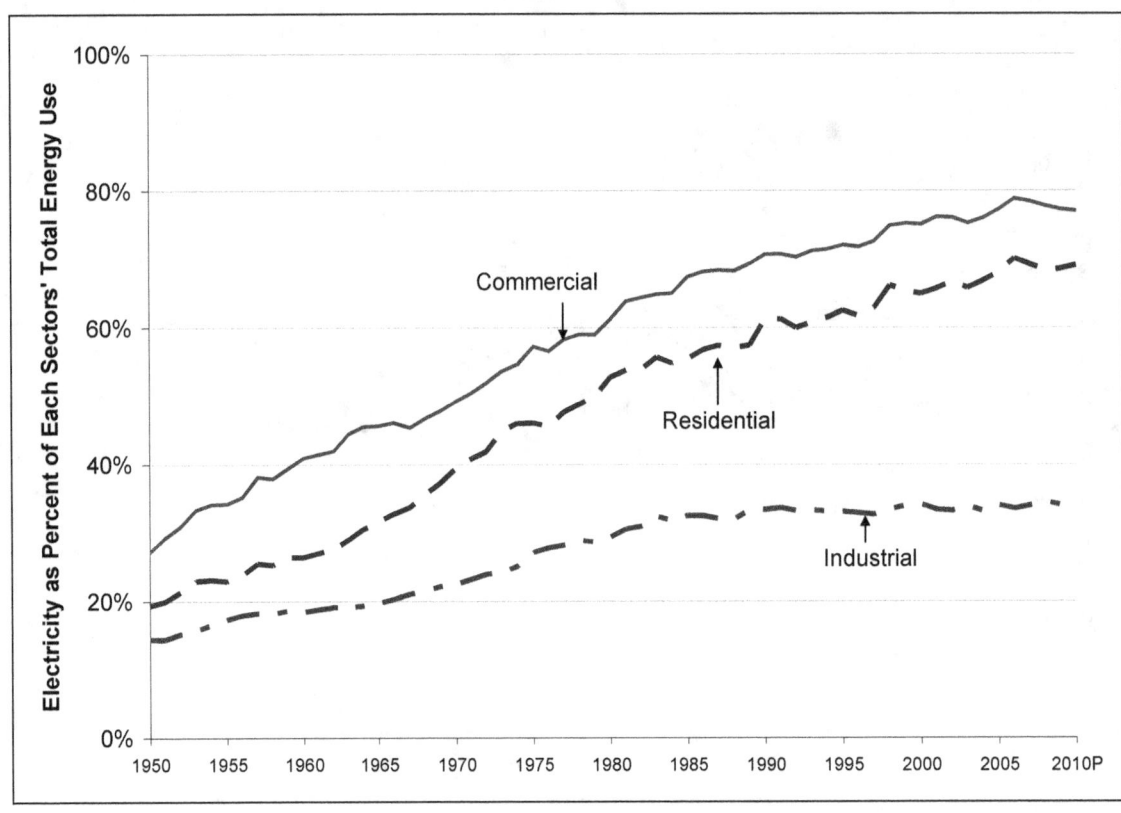

Source: Energy Information Administration (EIA), *Annual Energy Review 2010*, Tables 2.1a and D1. Per capita data calculated by CRS.

Notes: Data for 2010 are preliminary.

Consumption of major energy resources—petroleum, natural gas, and coal, as well as nuclear and renewable energy—is presented in **Table 2** and **Figure 3**. The historical trends show that petroleum has been and continues to be the major source of energy, rising from about 38% in 1950 to 45% in 1975, then declining to about 40% in response to the energy crisis of the 1970s. Natural gas followed a similar pattern at a lower level, increasing its share of total energy from about 17% in 1950 to over 30% in 1970, then declining to about 20%. Consumption of coal in 1950 was 35% of the total, almost equal to oil, but it declined to about 20% a decade later and has remained at about that proportion since then.

Table 2. Energy Consumption in British Thermal Units (Btu) and as a Percentage of Total, 1950-2010
(Quadrillion BTU)

	Petroleum		Natural Gas		Coal		Other		
	Quads	% of total	Quads	% of total	Quads	% of total	Quads	% of total	Total
1950	13.3	38.5%	6.0	17.2%	12.3	35.7%	3.0	8.6%	34.6
1955	17.3	42.9%	9.0	22.4%	11.2	27.7%	2.8	7.0%	40.2
1960	19.9	44.2%	12.4	27.5%	9.8	21.8%	2.9	6.5%	45.1
1965	23.2	43.0%	15.8	29.2%	11.6	21.4%	3.4	6.4%	54.0
1970	29.5	43.5%	21.8	32.1%	12.2	18.0%	4.3	6.4%	67.8
1975	32.7	45.5%	19.9	27.7%	12.7	17.6%	6.6	9.2%	72.0
1980	34.2	43.8%	20.2	25.9%	15.4	19.7%	8.2	10.6%	78.1
1985	30.9	40.5%	17.7	23.2%	17.5	22.9%	10.3	13.5%	76.4
1990	33.6	39.7%	19.6	23.2%	19.2	22.7%	12.2	14.4%	84.5
1995	34.4	37.8%	22.7	24.9%	20.1	22.1%	13.8	15.1%	91.0
2000	38.3	38.7%	23.8	24.1%	22.6	22.9%	14.1	14.3%	98.8
2005	40.4	40.3%	22.6	22.5%	22.8	22.8%	14.5	14.4%	100.3
2010P	36.0	36.7%	24.6	25.1%	20.8	21.2%	16.6	16.9%	98.0

Source: EIA, *Annual Energy Review 2010*, Table 1.3.

Notes: Percentages calculated by CRS. "Other" includes nuclear and renewable energy. Data for 2010 are preliminary.

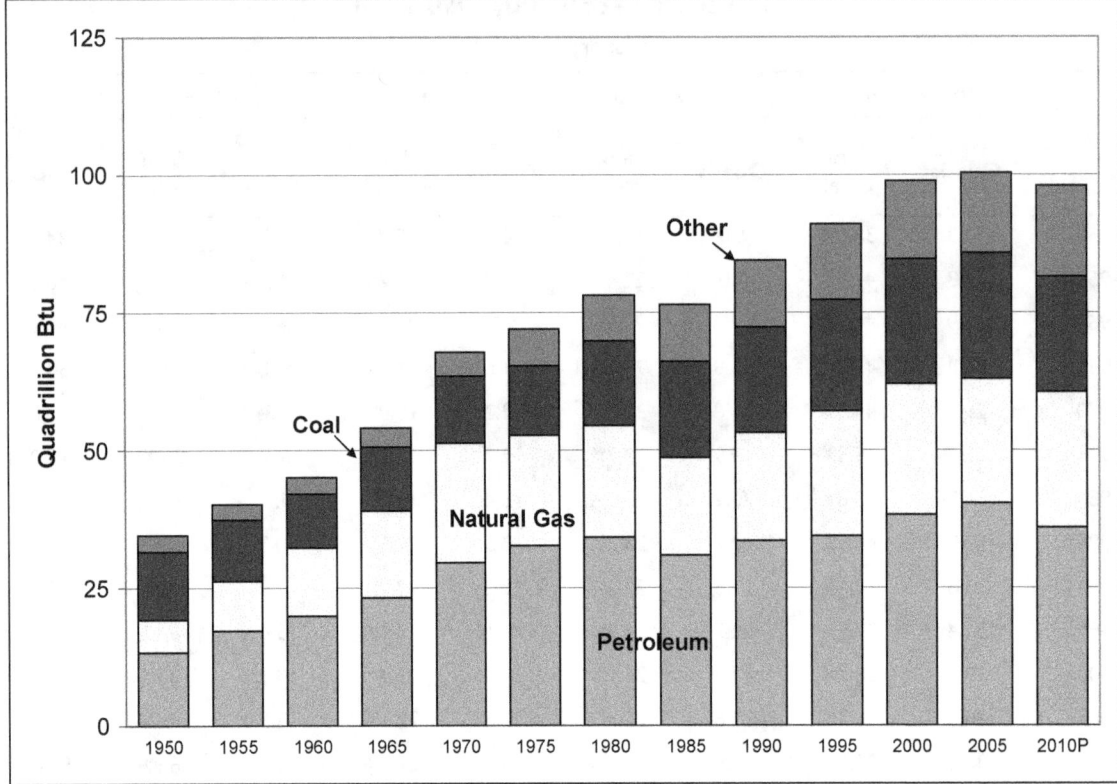

Figure 3. U.S. Energy Consumption by Source of Fuel, 1950-2010

Source: EIA, *Annual Energy Review 2010*, Table 1.3.

Notes: "Other" includes nuclear and renewable energy. Data for 2010 are preliminary.

Oil

About 40% of the energy consumed in the United States is supplied by petroleum, and that proportion has remained approximately the same since 1950, as the data in the previous section show. Also unchanged is the almost total dependence of the transportation sector on petroleum, mostly gasoline.

The perception that the world is on the verge of running out of oil, widespread during the 1970s, has changed, however. The rapid price increases at that time, aided by improved exploration and production technology, stimulated a global search for oil and resulted in the discovery of large amounts of new reserves. Indeed, as concerns about tightening supply and continually increasing prices were at a peak, and world production of petroleum grew, proven reserves actually increased by about 50% between 1973 and 1990. Some of the increase was in the Western Hemisphere, mostly in Mexico, but most was located in the region that already dominated the world oil market, the Middle East. With prices essentially steady during the 1990s, the search for oil slowed, but additions to reserves during the decade exceeded the amount of oil pumped out of the ground. By 2003, improved technology for retrieving petroleum from oil sands in Canada and, to a lesser extent, from heavy oil in Venezuela led to significant production from these resources, and by 2005, approximately 200 billion barrels of resources from oil sands and heavy oil were added to the total of proven world reserves, 20% of the total 1991 figure. In more recent years, successful extraction of tight oil (also called "shale oil") in the United States is likely to add significantly to world resources estimates. These trends are illustrated in **Figure 4.**

Figure 4. World Crude Oil Reserves, 1973, 1991, and 2008

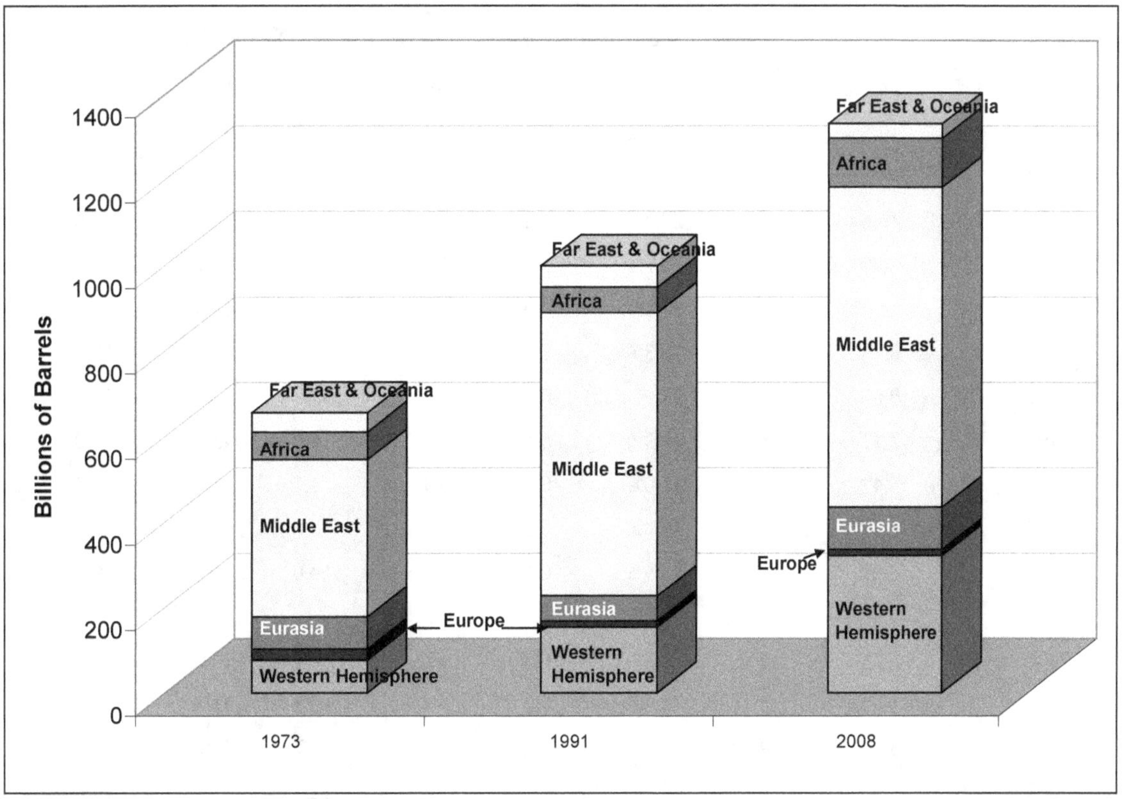

Source: EIA, *International Energy Annual (IEA) 1990*, Table 32 and *IEA 2007* Table 8.1 Table of World Proved Oil and Natural Gas Reserves, Most Recent Estimates. (data is from *Oil and Gas Journal* and is not certified by EIA, except for the data for the United States in the Western Hemisphere category).

Notes: The categories "Eastern Europe and Former Soviet Union" and "Western Europe," in the data for 1973 and 1991, were changed to "Eurasia" and "Europe" respectively for 2008. Seven countries (Albania, Bulgaria, Czech Republic, Hungary, Poland, Romania, and Slovakia) were moved from the former to the latter.

Petroleum Consumption, Supply, and Imports

Consumption of petroleum by sector reflects a variety of trends (see **Table 3**). In the residential and commercial sectors, petroleum consumption grew steadily from 1950 to 1970, while accounting for about 15% of total petroleum consumption. After the price surge in the 1970s, consumption in those sectors declined, falling to less than 7% of total petroleum consumption by 1995. When oil prices surged again after 2005, consumption declined further, to about 5%. Usage in the electric power sector followed a similar but more abrupt pattern. Until 1965 only about 3% of petroleum went to power generation. In the late 1960s efforts to improve air quality by reducing emissions led utilities to convert a number of coal-fired power plants to burn oil, and many new plants were designed to burn oil or natural gas. Utilities found themselves committed to increasing dependence on oil just at the time of shortages and high prices; in 1975 almost 9% of oil consumption went for power production. Consumption then fell sharply as alternate sources became available, declining to about 2%-3% of total consumption and falling even lower after 2005 as oil prices increased sharply.

Table 3. Petroleum Consumption by Sector, 1950-2010

(Million Barrels per Day (MBD) and Percentage of Total)

	Residential & Commercial		Industrial		Electric		Transportation		Total
	MBD	% of total	MBD	% of total	MBD	% of total	MBD	% of total	MBD
1950	1.1	16.5%	1.8	28.0%	0.2	3.2%	3.4	51.6%	6.5
1955	1.4	16.5%	2.4	28.1%	0.2	2.4%	4.5	52.4%	8.5
1960	1.7	17.5%	2.7	27.6%	0.2	2.5%	5.1	52.4%	9.8
1965	1.9	16.6%	3.2	27.2%	0.3	2.7%	6.0	52.5%	11.5
1970	2.2	14.9%	3.8	25.9%	0.9	6.3%	7.8	52.9%	14.7
1975	1.9	11.9%	4.0	24.8%	1.4	8.5%	9.0	54.9%	16.3
1980	1.5	8.9%	4.8	28.3%	1.2	6.7%	9.5	55.8%	17.1
1985	1.3	8.6%	4.1	25.9%	0.5	3.0%	9.8	62.7%	15.7
1990	1.2	7.2%	4.3	25.3%	0.6	3.3%	10.9	64.0%	17.0
1995	1.1	6.4%	4.6	26.0%	0.3	1.9%	11.7	65.9%	17.7
2000	1.3	6.5%	4.9	24.9%	0.5	2.6%	13.0	66.1%	19.7
2005	1.2	5.8%	5.1	24.5%	0.5	2.6%	14.0	67.1%	20.8
2006	1.1	5.2%	5.1	24.8%	0.3	1.4%	14.2	68.5%	20.7
2007	1.1	5.2%	5.1	24.4%	0.3	1.4%	14.3	69.0%	20.7
2008	1.1	5.5%	4.5	23.2%	0.2	1.1%	13.7	70.3%	19.5
2009	1.0	5.6%	4.3	22.8%	0.2	0.9%	13.3	70.7%	19.8
2010P	1.1	5.7%	4.4	22.9%	0.2	0.9%	13.5	70.5%	19.1

Source: EIA, *Annual Energy Review 2010*, Tables 5.11 and 5.13a-d.

Notes: Percentages calculated by CRS. Data for 2010 are preliminary.

Industrial consumption of petroleum, which includes such large consumers as refineries and petrochemical industries, has remained about 25% of total consumption since 1970. As other sectors' share fell, transportation, which was a little more than half of total consumption prior to 1975, climbed to two-thirds by 2000 and continued to increase its share since then. The slowing of the economy in the summer of 2008 led to a drop in total oil consumption in 2009.

While petroleum consumption increased throughout the period from 1950 to the present (except for a temporary decline following the price surge of the 1970s and another in 2009), U.S. domestic production peaked in 1970. However, in recent years expanded production of tight oil has reversed the decline in production. (See **Table 4**). The result, as shown in **Figure 5**, was greater dependence on imported petroleum, which rose from less than 20% in 1960 to near 60% in 2005. With a decline in consumption following 2008, and increased production, import dependence declined to about 45% in 2011.

Table 4. U.S. Petroleum Production, 1950-2010

(Million Barrels per Day)

	Crude Oil			Gas Liquids	Other	Total
	48 States	**Alaska**	**Total**			
1950	5.4	—	5.4	0.5	—	5.9
1955	6.8	—	6.8	0.8	—	7.6
1960	7	—	7	0.9	0.2	8.1
1965	7.8	—	7.8	1.2	0.2	9.2
1970	9.4	0.2	9.6	1.7	0.4	11.7
1975	8.2	0.2	8.4	1.6	0.5	10.5
1980	7	1.6	8.6	1.6	0.6	10.8
1985	7.2	1.8	9	1.6	0.6	11.1
1990	5.6	1.8	7.4	1.6	0.7	9.6
1995	5.1	1.5	6.6	1.8	0.8	9.1
2000	4.9	1.0	5.8	1.9	1.0	8.7
2005	4.3	0.9	5.2	1.7	1.0	7.9
2006	4.4	0.7	5.1	1.7	1.0	7.8
2007	4.3	0.7	5.1	1.8	1.0	8.9
2008	4.3	0.7	5.0	1.8	1.0	8.8
2009	4.7	0.6	5.4	1.9	1.7	9.0
2010P	4.9	0.6	5.5	2.0	2.0	9.5

Source: EIA, *Annual Energy Review 2010*, Table 5.1b.

Notes: "Other" includes processing gain. Data for 2010 are preliminary.

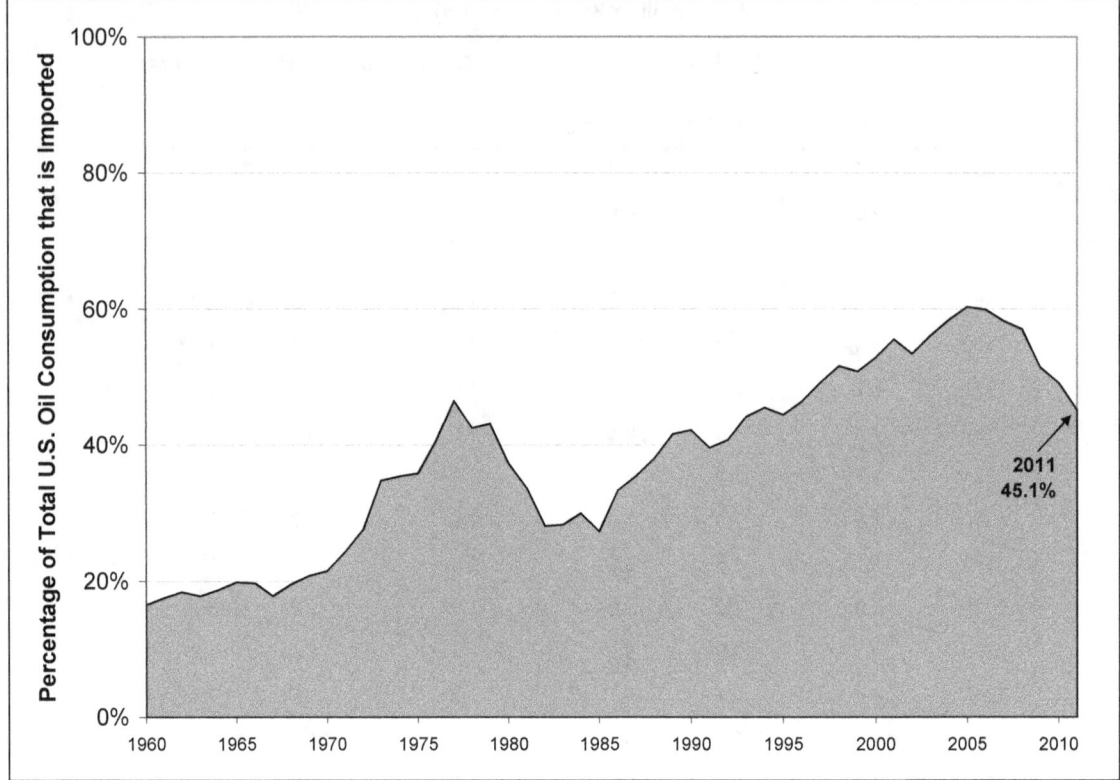

Figure 5. U.S. Consumption of Imported Petroleum, 1960-2011

Source: EIA, *Monthly Energy Review*, February 2012, Table 3.3a, and *Annual Energy Review 1986*, Table 51.

Petroleum and Transportation

Since the transportation sector is so heavily dependent on petroleum, and uses so much of it, **Table 5** and **Figure 6** present a more detailed breakdown of the various types of petroleum products used.

Table 5. Transportation Use of Petroleum, 1950-2010

(Million barrels per day)

	Aviation	Diesel Fuel	Gasoline	Other	Total
1950	0.1	0.2	2.4	0.6	3.4
1955	0.3	0.4	3.2	0.6	4.5
1960	0.5	0.4	3.7	0.5	5.1
1965	0.7	0.5	4.4	0.4	6.0
1970	1.0	0.7	5.6	0.5	7.8
1975	1.0	1.0	6.5	0.4	9.0
1980	1.1	1.3	6.4	0.7	9.5
1985	1.2	1.5	6.7	0.5	9.8
1990	1.5	1.7	7.1	0.6	10.9

	Aviation	Diesel Fuel	Gasoline	Other	Total
1995	1.5	2.0	7.7	0.5	11.7
2000	1.7	2.4	8.4	0.5	13.0
2005	1.7	2.9	8.9	0.5	14.0
2006	1.7	3.0	9.0	0.4	14.3
2007	1.6	3.0	9.1	0.5	14.3
2008	1.6	2.8	8.8	0.5	13.7
2009	1.4	2.6	8.8	0.4	13.3
2010P	1.4	2.7	8.9	0.5	13.5

Source: EIA, *Annual Energy Review 2010*, Table 5.13c.

Notes: Data for 2010 are preliminary.

Aviation fuel includes both aviation gasoline and kerosene jet fuel. In 1950 aviation was almost entirely gasoline powered; by 2000 it was 99% jet fueled. The growth in flying is illustrated by the fact that aviation fuel was only 3% of petroleum consumption for transportation in 1950, but had grown to 12% in 1965 and has maintained that share since then.

Diesel fuel consumption showed a similar dramatic increase. About 6% of total petroleum consumption for transportation in 1950, it rose to 11% by 1975 and to 20% in recent years. Diesel fuel is used by a number of transportation sectors. Part of the increase involved the change of railroads from coal-fired steam to diesel and diesel-electric power. Diesel fuel is used also in the marine transportation sector, and some private automobiles are diesel-powered. The major part of diesel fuel consumption in transportation is by large commercial trucks. Total diesel fuel consumption increased from about 200,000 barrels per day in 1950 to 3.0 million barrels per day in 2007. The economic downturn in 2008 led to a decline in diesel consumption.

Most of the petroleum consumed in the transportation sector is motor gasoline. In 1950 it was 71% of total sector petroleum consumption, and in recent years, despite the increase in aviation fuel and diesel, it has been about 65%. Since 1950, gasoline consumption has almost quadrupled. Like diesel fuel, gasoline consumption fell after the economic decline in the summer of 2008.

Of the other petroleum products consumed in the transportation sector, the largest is residual fuel oil, most of which is used in large marine transport. Consumption of residual fuel oil in the transportation sector was about 500,000 barrels in 1950, and declined gradually to about 400,000 in 2000.

Figure 6. Transportation Use of Petroleum, 1950-2010

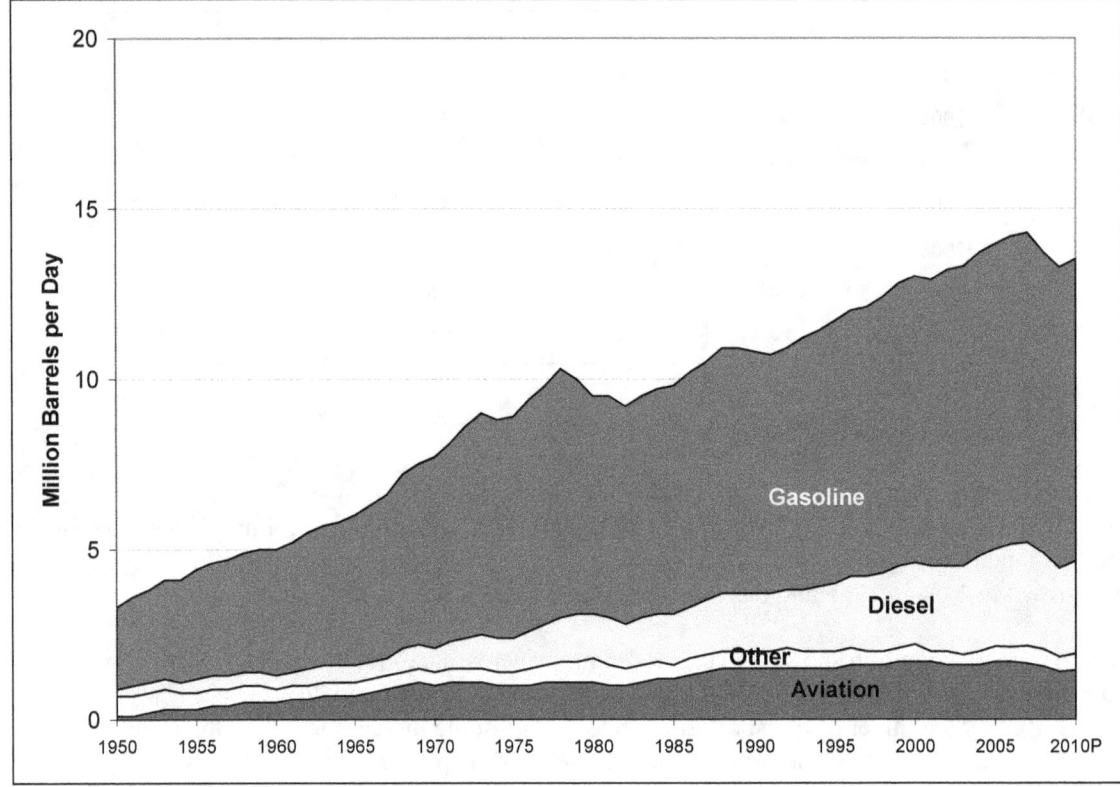

Source: EIA, *Annual Energy Review 2010*, Table 5.13c.

Notes: Data for 2010 are preliminary.

Petroleum Prices: Historical Trends

Most commodity prices are volatile. Because oil is widely consumed, and is so important at all levels of the economy, its price is closely watched and analyzed. Especially since the 1970s, when a generally stable market dominated by a few large oil companies was broken by the Organization of the Petroleum Exporting Countries (OPEC) cartel and a relatively open world market came into being, the price of crude oil has been particularly volatile. **Figure 7** and **Figure 8** show the long-term trends of crude oil and gasoline prices, in both current dollars and deflated dollars.

Figure 7. Nominal and Real Cost of Crude Oil to Refiners, 1968-2010

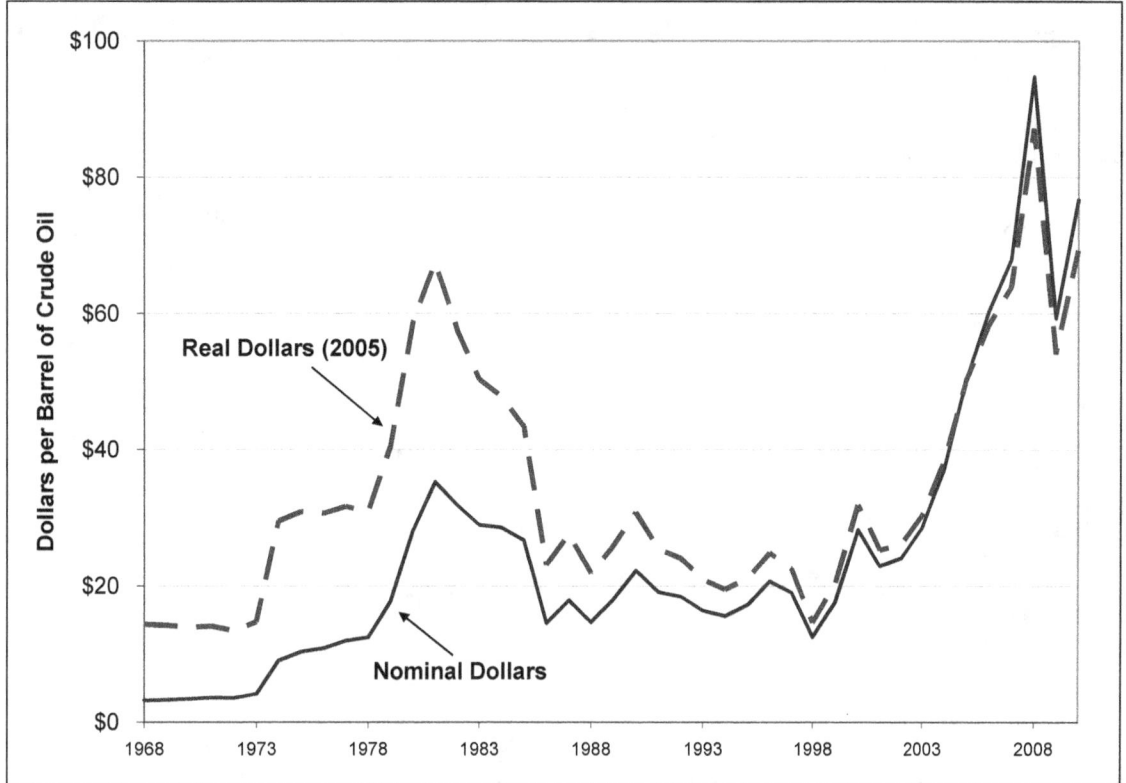

Source: EIA, *Annual Energy Review 2010*, Table 5.21.

Notes: Costs are for crude oil to refiners, including transportation and other fees; they do not include crude oil purchased for the Strategic Petroleum Reserve. Data for 2010 are preliminary.

At the consumer level, prices of products such as motor gasoline and heating oil have reacted to price and supply disruptions in ways that have been modulated by various government and industry policies and international events. A significant and not often noted fact is that, like many commodities, the long-term trend in gasoline prices, adjusted for inflation and excluding temporary surges, has been down. As shown in **Figure 8**, the real price of gasoline peaked in 1980, then fell precipitously in the mid-1980s. The surge in prices that peaked in 2008 brought the price above the peak of 1980 (in real dollars).

Figure 8. Nominal and Real Price of Gasoline, 1950-2010

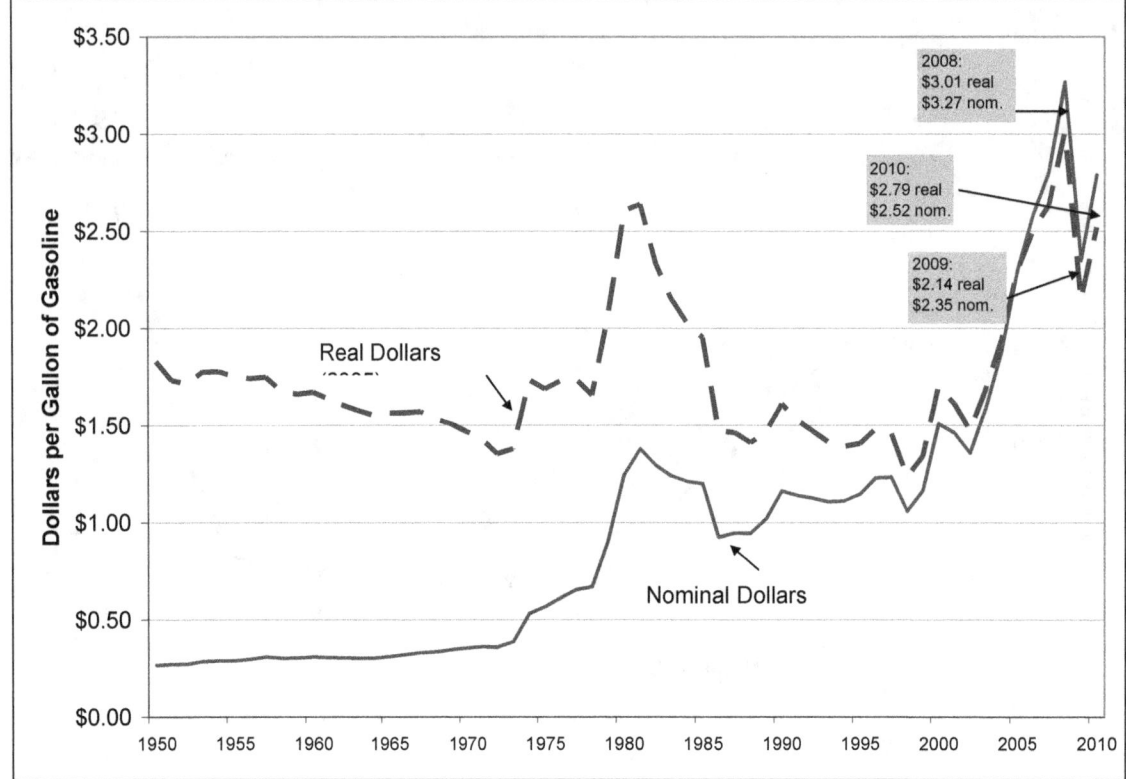

Source: EIA, *Annual Energy Review 2010*, Table 5.24,

Notes: Average national retail price per gallon of unleaded regular gasoline, including taxes.

Figure 9 illustrates the proportion of the gross domestic product (GDP) dedicated to consumer spending on oil. The price surges in the 1970s pushed this ratio from about 4.5% before the Arab oil embargo to about 8.5% following the crisis in Iran late in the decade. Following that, it declined to less than 4%. During the recent run-up of prices the trend started back up again, reaching 6% in 2008, and falling in 2009.

Figure 9. Consumer Spending on Oil as a Percentage of GDP, 1970-2009

Source: EIA, *Annual Energy Review 2010*, Table 3.5 and Table D1 for GDP in billions of nominal dollars. Percentages calculated by CRS.

Petroleum Prices: The 2004-2008 Bubble and Back Up Again

Beginning in 2004 the world price of crude oil, and with it the price of gasoline, began to increase. Unlike the previous increases in the 1970s, there was no interruption or shortage in the supply of either petroleum or its products, except for a few months in the fall of 2005 when Hurricane Katrina shut down a major portion of U.S. refinery capacity as well as some crude oil production and delivery capacity. Nevertheless, an unexpected surge in demand for oil imports to China, added to continuing increases in demand from Europe and the United States as economies continued to grow, tightened the production capacity of the major oil producing nations and signaled that demand in the near future might not be met. In addition, turmoil in the Middle East and elsewhere, as well as the possibility of further natural disasters like Katrina, threatened supply interruptions and put further upward pressure on prices. (See **Figure 10** and **Figure 11**.)

As prices continued to climb, it became apparent that demand for gasoline was relatively insensitive to its cost to the consumer. Throughout the period, as illustrated in **Figure 12**, consumption of gasoline varied seasonally but continued an upward trend on an annual basis. In the summer of 2008 crude oil prices soared far beyond the actual cost of production, and the market took on features of a classical commodities bubble, with expectations of indefinitely rising prices and participation in the market by many who would not normally enter it.

The bubble burst in October 2008 with the onset of a financial crisis in the housing and banking sectors and the evidence that consumption of gasoline was finally faltering. As the economic crisis became more acute, crude prices fell in a few months from $135 per barrel to close to $40, where they had been at the start of the run-up five years earlier.

At the end of 2010, with the economy beginning to recover, oil prices began to rise again. When unrest in Libya, a major oil producer, interrupted some supply to Europe, prices of both crude oil and gasoline surged again. As that crisis eased, prices fell, only to rise again with an impending prospect of a supply interruption involving Iran.[4]

Figure 10. Crude Oil Futures Prices January 2000 to March 2012

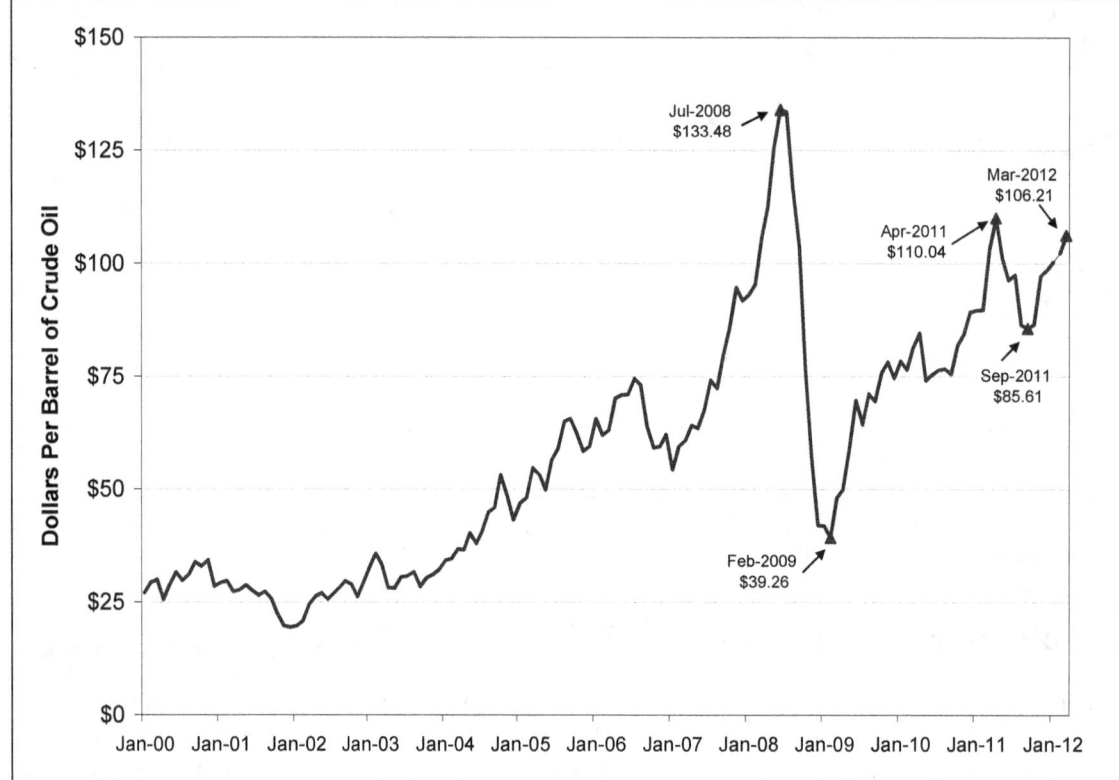

Source: EIA, NYMEX Futures Prices Crude Oil (Light-Sweet, Cushing, Oklahoma) Cushing, OK Crude Oil Future Contract 1.

Notes: The futures prices shown are the official daily closing prices at 2:30 p.m. from the trading floor of the New York Mercantile Exchange (NYMEX) for a specific delivery month for each product listed. Last date above is March 2012; $106.21. February 2012 was $102.26 / barrel.

---

[4] For detailed analysis of trends and policies concerning gasoline prices, see CRS Report R42382, *Rising Gasoline Prices 2012*, by Neelesh Nerurkar and Robert Pirog.

**Figure 11. Average Daily Nationwide Price of Unleaded Gasoline
January 2002-April 2012**

Source: Daily Fuel Gauge Report, American Automobile Association, http://www.fuelgaugereport.com, compiled by CRS.

Notes: Prices include federal, state, and local taxes. Last date above is April 11, 2012; $3.92.

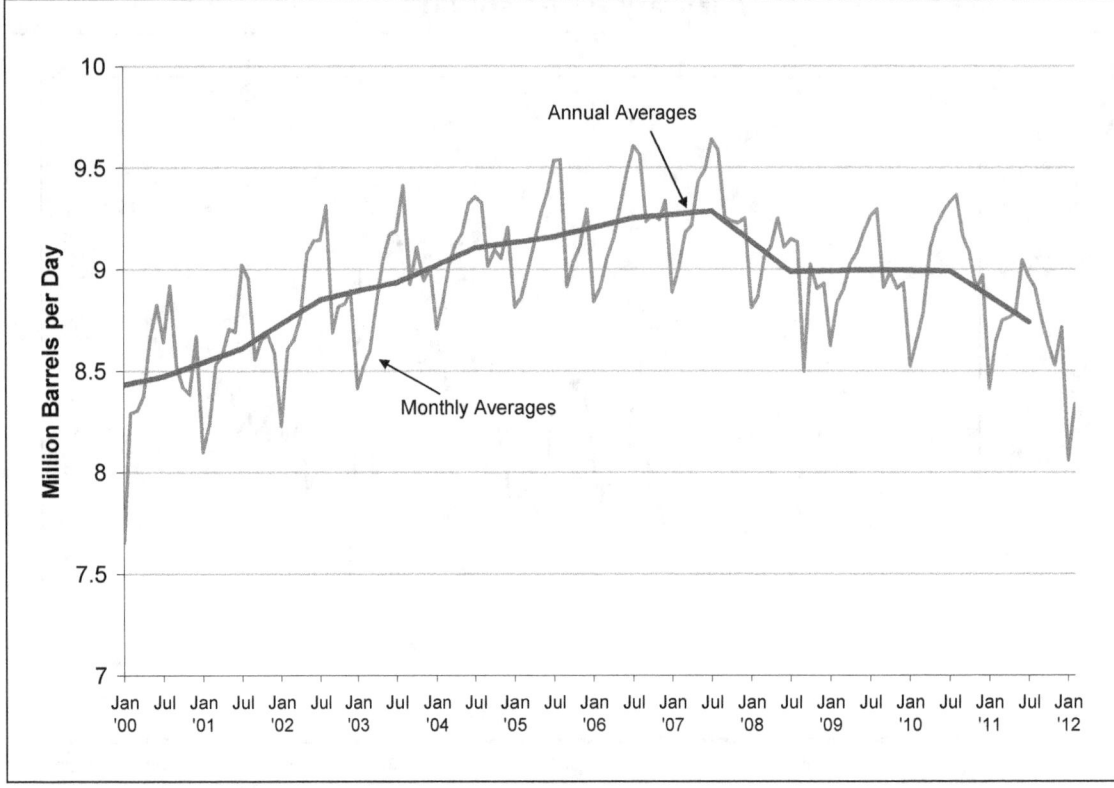

Figure 12. U.S. Gasoline Consumption, January 2000-March 2012

Source: EIA, *Monthly Energy Review*, March 2012, Table 3.5, and EIA, *Weekly Petroleum Status Report.* 4/11/12, Table A1.

Note: Some of the data points in the chart above are as follows: Average for 2010 = 9.0, Estimated Average for 2011 = 8.7, Estimated Averages for January 2012 = 8.1, for February = 8.3, and for March = 8.6.

Why Are Oil Prices So High?[5]

Many diverse factors combine to determine prices in a world oil market that is globally integrated. About 60% of the world's oil supply is traded internationally, and particular sources of oil can be interchangeable within the limits set by the oil's quality. Consequently, the price of oil is global. No matter where it is produced or consumed, the price tends to move in the same direction at a similar rate. New supplies, or disruptions to existing supplies, will impact prices around the world, no matter where those events occur. Similarly, a change in demand in any particular country is likely to affect prices globally.

The price of oil generally increased from 2003 until peaking at $145 per barrel in mid-2008. This run-up of oil prices was unlike the two oil crises in the 1970s, in that there was no major interruption of supply. In 1973-1974, Arab members of the Organization of the Petroleum Exporting Countries (OPEC) embargoed shipments of oil to the United States and the Netherlands because of their support of Israel during the Yom Kippur War. The resulting shortages, coupled with domestic price controls in the United States, led to lines at gas stations

---

[5] For a detailed analysis of oil prices, see CRS Report 42024, *Oil Price Fluctuations,* by Neelesh Nerurkar, and Mark Jickling.

and widespread concern about energy security. During the later disruption in oil supply following the Iranian revolution in 1979, the shortages and gas station lines were so severe that Congress began considering a gasoline rationing plan.

However, there was no period during 2003 to 2008 when oil was in short supply, except for a brief period following Hurricane Katrina in 2005, and there were no lines at the gas pumps, except for a limited time in a few places. Nevertheless, the price of oil climbed steadily during that period. As it climbed, so did the price of gasoline. But despite the higher price, consumption of gasoline continued to increase, indicating that consumers were relatively insensitive to the increased cost. Only when the economy began to falter in the summer of 2008 did consumption significantly decline. Once the U.S. recession spread to the rest of the world in 2008, global oil consumption and prices collapsed, falling to a one-day low of less than $31 per barrel.

Within a year of the 2008 collapse, the price of oil recovered to the range of $70-$85, far above the $20-$30 region it had been in during the 15 years previous to the price run-up. (See **Figure 7** for long-term yearly average prices, and **Figure 10** for more current weekly average price movements.) Significantly, the actual cost of producing most of the oil currently being supplied to the market had not risen to a degree comparable to the increase in price. The question then arises, why are oil prices so much higher than they were in the 1990s?

Numerous factors in addition to the current cost of production contribute to the price of oil. First, a major feature of the oil market is that very large capital investments, and considerable time, are necessary to bring known resources into production. Investors in production facilities as a result are interested not only in current demand and supply, but in expectations as to how demand and supply will change in the future. Second, not only market factors but political decisions play a major role in determining the price of oil, especially since many of the world's primary producers are nationally owned. In many of those countries where oil is state-owned, oil revenue is often treated as part of the general revenue, and devoted to governmental purposes rather than enhancing the production capacity of the oil industry.

These are only two of the many factors that influence oil prices. Specifically, the following factors may be important:

- **Geopolitical Factors, Including OPEC.** The concentration of oil resources in the Persian Gulf countries means that the political events in the Middle East can have great influence on the oil market. Their influence is enhanced by the monopolistic policies of OPEC, which is dominated by Saudi Arabia and other Persian Gulf countries. Also contributing to the importance of this factor is the resource nationalism of government-owned oil companies, noted above, and the practice of many developing countries, where demand growth has become rapid, to subsidize gasoline consumption with regulated low prices.

- **A Changing Market.** To an increasing degree, investors in oil futures have been investors with little interest in oil as a commodity, such as investment banks and pension and endowment funds. A debatable question is the degree to which such investors lead to a market focused more on future prospects than present conditions.

- **Inelastic Demand for Oil Products, Particularly Gasoline.** During the 2003-2008 run-up of prices, U.S. consumption of gasoline continued to increase, indicating that consumers were relatively insensitive to what it cost to keep their automobiles running. Only when the economy faltered in the summer of 2008 did consumption decline. The insensitivity to price is exacerbated in some countries, particularly in the developing nations and the oil-exporting countries, by government subsidies noted above, which mask the actual cost of gasoline.

- **Foreign Exchange Rates.** Oil is traded in dollars, even in foreign markets. As a result, changes in the value of the dollar relative to other currencies can have an effect on the price of oil.

- **Changing Views on Oil Resources.** Because the oil market is forward-looking, future supply and demand conditions are important factors in determining price. During the crises of the 1970s, there was a widespread belief that natural resources in general, including oil, were running out.[6] In the 1980s, after the price of oil collapsed in the face of reduced demand and excess production capacity, the limits to growth concept lost much of its support. However, during the recent price run-up, there was, and continues to be, widespread belief that future finds of large oil deposits will diminish, and even that world oil production will soon reach a peak and stabilize or decline. These predictions are controversial — they appear to be contradicted by the doubling of world proven oil reserves, as shown in **Figure 4** — but they have a powerful influence on the forward-looking oil market.

Gasoline Taxes

The federal tax on gasoline is currently 18.4 cents per gallon. An extensive list of the gasoline and diesel fuel tax rates imposed by each state per gallon of motor fuel is maintained and updated by the American Petroleum Institute (API), "Notes to State Motor Fuel Excise and Other Tax Rates," at http://www.api.org/Oil-and-Natural-Gas-Overview/Industry-Economics/~/media/Files/Statistics/State_Motor_Fuel_Excise_Tax_Update.ashx.

Electricity

While overall energy consumption in the United States increased nearly three-fold since 1950, electricity consumption increased even more rapidly. Annual power generation is ten times what it was in 1950. **Figure 13** illustrates the trend.

---

[6] An important expression of this view was a study by the Club of Rome: Donella H. Meadows, Dennis L. Meadows, Jorgen Randers, and William W. Behrens III. *The Limits to Growth.* New York: Universe Books (1972).

Figure 13. Electricity Generation by Source, Selected Years, 1950-2010

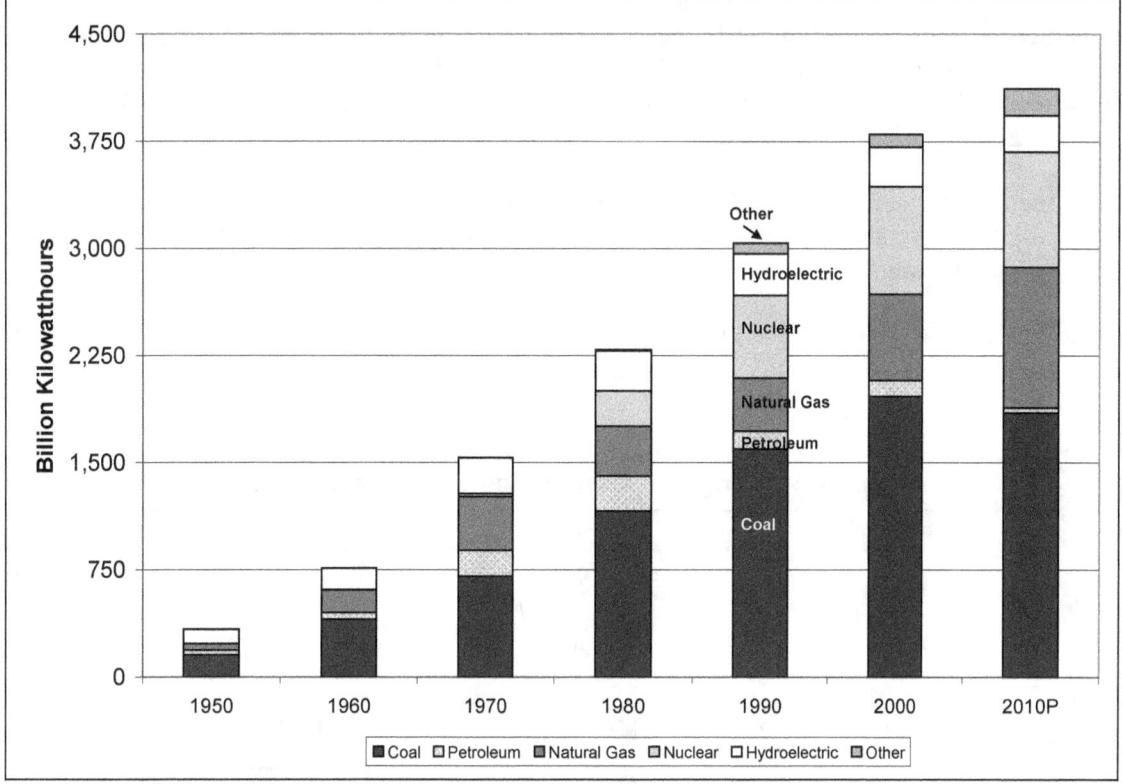

Source: EIA, *Annual Energy Review 2010*, Table 8.2a.

Throughout this period, coal was used to generate about half the rapidly increasing amount of electricity consumed. Petroleum became briefly important as a source of power generation in the late 1960s because it resulted in lower emissions of air pollutants, and consumption continued in the 1970s despite the price surge because natural gas was in short supply. By the 1980s, however, oil consumption by utilities dropped sharply, and in 2010 less than 1% of power generation was oil-fired.

Natural gas generation has a more complicated history. Consumption by the electric power industry increased gradually as access by pipeline became more widespread. With the price increase in oil in the 1970s, demand for gas also increased, but interstate prices were regulated, and gas availability declined. In addition, federal energy policy viewed generation of electricity by gas to be a wasteful use of a diminishing resource. The Fuel Use Act of 1978 prohibited new power generators from using gas and set a timetable for shutting down existing gas-fired plants. Gas prices were later deregulated, resulting in increased production, and the Fuel Use Act was repealed, but in the meantime generation of electricity from gas fell from 24% in 1970 to 12% in 1985. In the 1990s gas became more popular as technology improved, and as electricity producers faced tighter Clean Air Act requirements. By 2000 16% of total electric generation was gas-fired, and by 2011 the figure reached 25%. Most capacity additions since 1995 have been gas-fired, as illustrated in **Figure 14**.

Nuclear power started coming on line in significant amounts in the late 1960s, and by 1975, in the midst of the oil crisis, was supplying 9% of total generation. However, increases in capital costs, construction delays, and public opposition to nuclear power following the Three Mile Island accident in 1979 curtailed expansion of the technology, and many construction projects were cancelled. Continuation of some construction increased the nuclear share of generation to 20% in 1990, where it remains currently. Recently, some new projects have entered the licensing and construction stage, but the future of nuclear power remains in question. The accident at Fukushima in March 2011 contributed a further factor entering decisions regarding future construction. (For more details on U.S. nuclear power activity, see CRS Report RL33558, *Nuclear Energy Policy*, by Mark Holt.)

Construction of major hydroelectric projects has also essentially ceased, and hydropower's share of electricity generation has gradually declined from 30% in 1950 to 15% in 1975 and less than 10% in 2000. However, hydropower remains highly important on a regional basis.

In the last decade, a new trend has begun: the addition of wind energy. As **Figure 14** illustrates, more than 30 gigawatts of wind energy electricity generating capacity has been added to the U.S. power grid since 2003.

Figure 14. Changes in Generating Capacity, 1995-2010

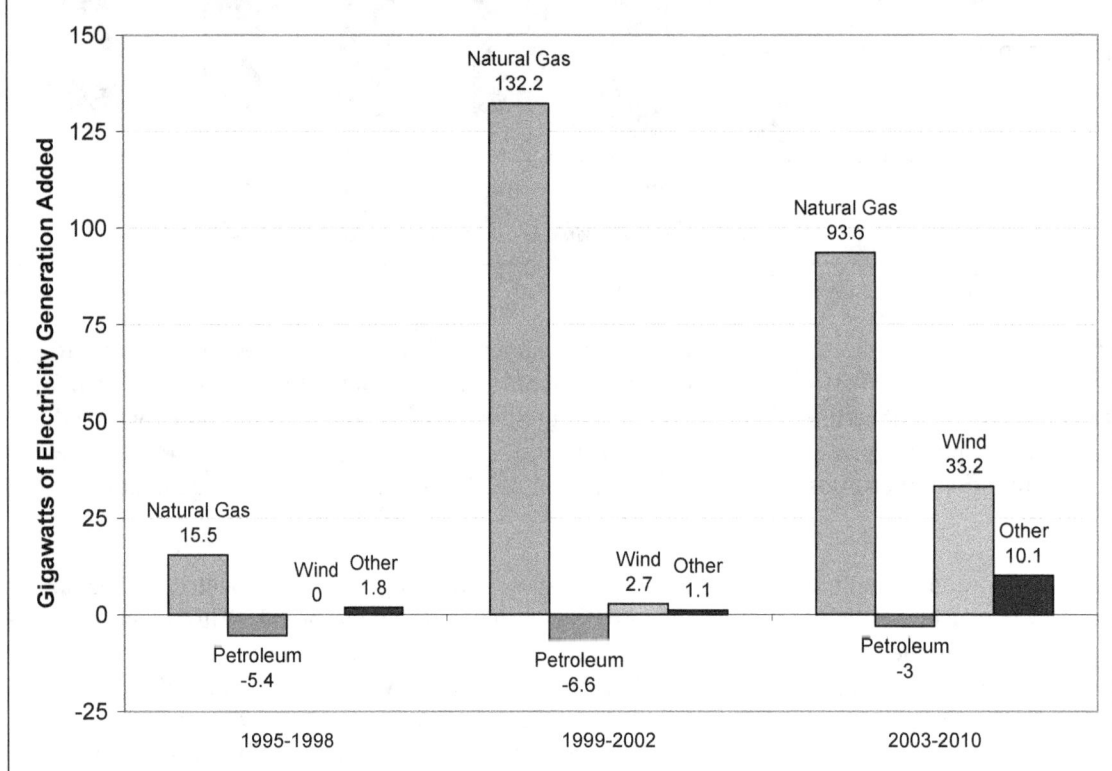

Source: EIA, *Annual Energy Review 2010*, Table 8.11a.

Note: Other is coal, nuclear, hydro and other renewables excluding wind. Data for 2010 are preliminary.

Sources of power generation vary greatly by region (see **Table 6**). Hydropower in the Pacific Coast states, for instance, supplies over 40% of total generation, and natural gas almost 35%. Other regions are heavily dependent on coal generation: The North Central and East South Central states, as well as the Mountain states, generate more than 60% of their electricity from coal, whereas other regions, such as New England and the Pacific Coast, use relatively little coal. The West South Central region (Arkansas, Louisiana, Oklahoma, and Texas) generates 45% of its electricity from gas. New England in the 1970s and 1980s was heavily dependent on oil-generated power; in 2005, despite an increased use of natural gas, oil produced 10% of New England's power, compared with the national average of 2.5%. By 2011, the proportion had dropped to less than 1%, and more than half New England's electric power was generated by gas.

Table 6. Electricity Generation by Region and Fuel, 2011

	Total Generation	Percentage by					
	(billion kwh)	Coal	Petroleum	Natural Gas	Nuclear	Hydro	Other
New England	123.4	5.8 %	0.5 %	51.6 %	27.8 %	6.7 %	7.6 %
Middle Atlantic	430.0	26.7 %	0.3 %	27.4 %	35.5 %	7.1 %	3.0 %
East North Central	628.9	63.4 %	0.1 %	7.5 %	24.7 %	0.9 %	3.4 %
West North Central	333.1	69.4 %	0.1 %	3.7 %	12.2 %	4.4 %	10.2 %
South Atlantic	765.1	42.6 %	0.4 %	28.1 %	24.5 %	1.9 %	2.5 %
East South Central	387.9	51.3 %	0.1 %	21.3 %	19.8 %	5.6 %	1.8 %
West South Central	678.9	36.3 %	0.0 %	44.6 %	10.4 %	1.1 %	7.6 %
Mountain	363.4	54.7 %	0.1 %	19.6 %	8.6 %	11.4 %	5.6 %
Pacific Contiguous	377.7	2.8 %	0.0 %	26.6 %	11.0 %	47.5 %	12.1 %
Pacific Noncontiguous	17.2	11.8 %	50.6 %	21.5 %	0.0%	10.0 %	6.2 %
U.S. Total	4,105.7	42.2 %	0.4 %	24.8 %	19.2 %	7.9 %	5.4 %

Source: EIA, *Electric Power Monthly*, February 2012, Tables 1.6B, 1.7B, 1.8B, 1.10B, 1.12B, and 1.13B.

Note: "Other" includes renewables other than hydro, plus hydro from pumped storage, petroleum coke, gases other than natural gas, and other sources.

The price of electricity varies by region, depending on the fuel mix and the local regulatory system, among other factors. The nationwide average retail price to residential consumers increased during the 1970s energy crises but declined starting in the 1980s, as indicated by **Figure 15**. An increase starting in 2000 resulted from the expiration in numerous regions of price caps that had been previously imposed when utilities were deregulated. By 2010 prices had begun to level off again, in part because of the falling cost of natural gas to utilities (see **Figure 16**).

Figure 15. Price of Retail Residential Electricity, 1960-2010

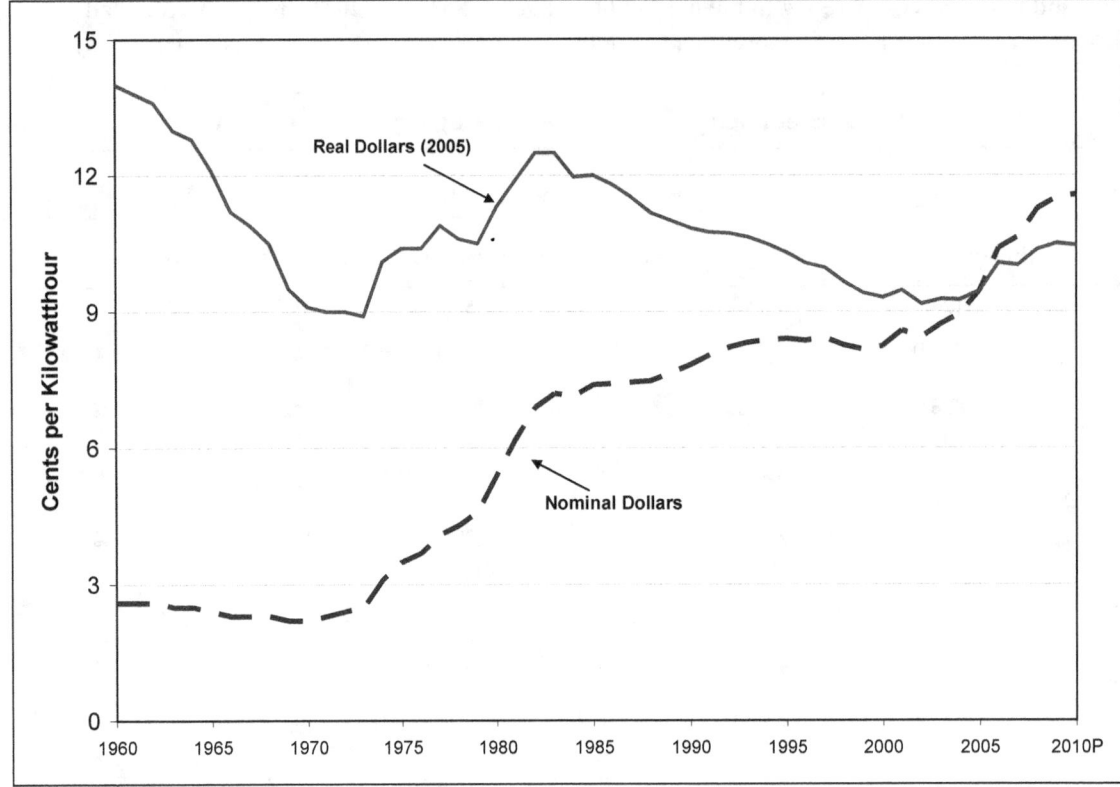

Source: EIA, *Annual Energy Review 2010*, Table 8.10.

Notes: Price includes taxes. Data for 2010 are preliminary.

Other Conventional Energy Resources

Natural Gas

Consumption of natural gas was more than four times as great in 2010 as it was in 1950. Throughout the period, consumption in the residential and commercial sector grew at about the same rate as total consumption, in the range of 30% to 40% of the total. As shown in **Table 7**, consumption for electric power generation increased from about 10% in 1950 to more than 20% at the end of the century and 30% by 2010. The proportion of total gas consumption by the industrial sector declined correspondingly, from more than 50% in 1950 to about 33% in recent years.

Table 7. Natural Gas Consumption by Sector, 1950-2010

	Total Consumption	Percent Consumed by Sector		
	trillion cubic feet (tcf)	Residential - Commercial	Industrial	Electric
1950	5.77	27.5%	59.4%	10.9%
1955	8.69	31.7%	52.2%	13.3%
1960	11.97	34.5%	48.2%	14.4%
1965	15.28	35.0%	46.5%	15.2%
1970	21.14	34.2%	43.8%	18.6%
1975	19.54	38.0%	42.8%	16.2%
1980	19.88	37.0%	41.2%	18.5%
1985	17.28	39.7%	39.7%	17.6%
1990	19.17	36.6%	43.1%	16.9%
1995	22.21	35.5%	42.3%	19.1%
2000	23.33	35.0%	39.8%	22.3%
2005	22.01	35.6%	35.0%	26.7%
2006	21.69	33.2%	35.3%	28.7%
2007	23.10	33.5%	34.1%	29.7%
2008	23.27	34.6%	33.9%	28.7%
2009	22.84	34.6%	32.6%	30.1%
2010P	24.13	33.8%	32.9%	30.6%

Source: EIA, *Annual Energy Review 2010*, Table 6.5.

Notes: Data for 2010 are preliminary. Percentages do not add to 100. The remaining amount is used by the transportation sector.

In part because of increased demand by electric utilities, natural gas prices have become extremely volatile in recent years, as illustrated by **Figure 16**, which shows high, low, and yearly average prices for gas delivered to electricity generators. The recent boom in production of shale gas has led to an oversupply and consequently lower prices.

Figure 16. Natural Gas Prices to Electricity Generators, 1978-2010

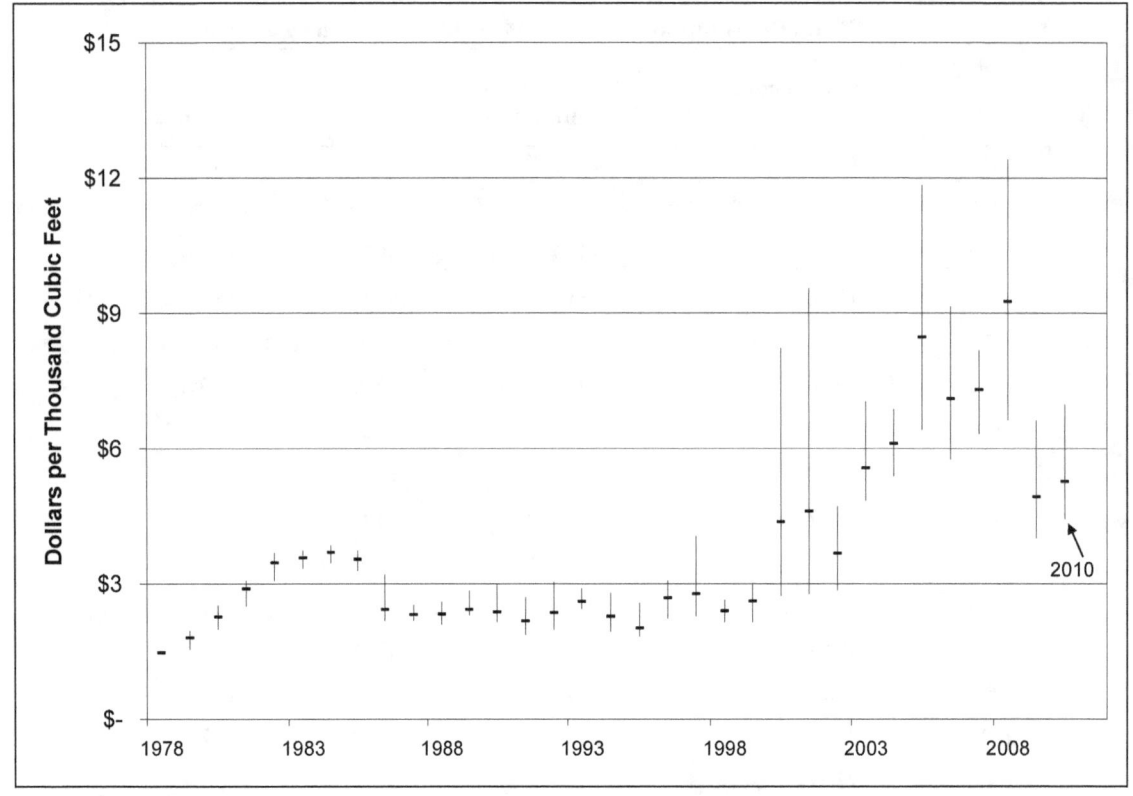

Source: EIA, *Monthly Energy Review*, December 2011, Table 9.11.

Rates for residential natural gas are regulated, but local gas companies are usually allowed to pass fuel costs through to customers, so there is considerable seasonal fluctuation as winter heating demand increases consumption, as shown in **Figure 17**. The long-term trend in residential natural gas prices, both in current dollars and in constant 2008 dollars, is shown in **Figure 18**.

Figure 17. Monthly and Annual Residential Natural Gas Prices, 2000-November 2011

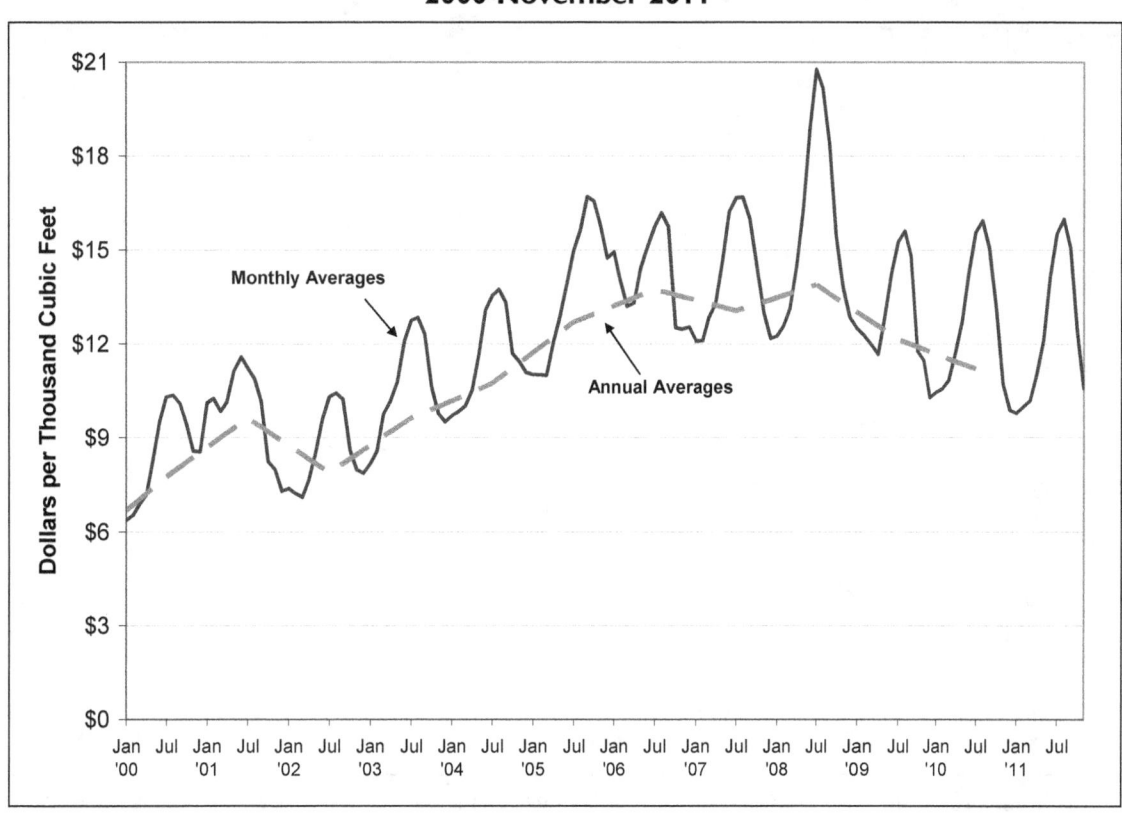

Source: EIA, *Monthly Energy Review*, February 2012, Table 9.11.

Figure 18. Annual Residential Natural Gas Prices, 1973-2010

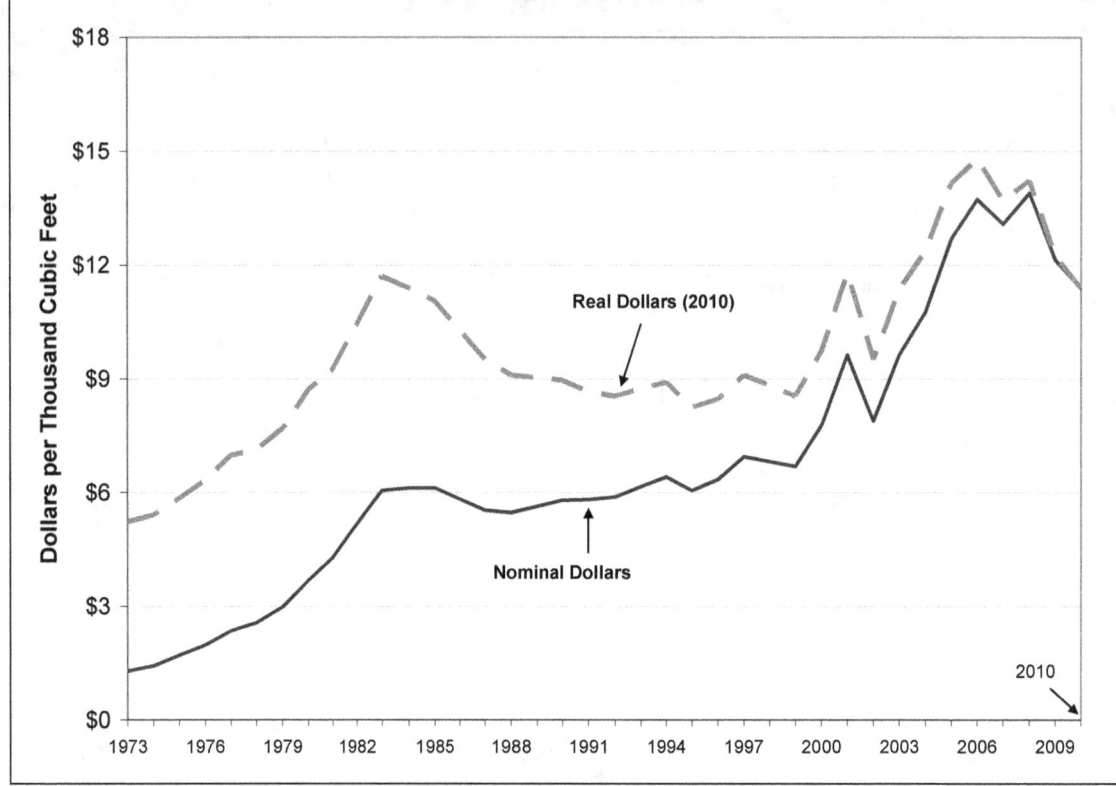

Source: EIA, *Monthly Energy Review*, September 2010, Table 9.11 and FY2013 Budget, *Historical Tables*, Table 10.1 for GDP Chained Price Index.

Coal

Consumption of coal has more than doubled since 1950, but during that period coal as an energy source changed from a widely used resource to a single-use fuel for generating electricity. (See **Table 7.**) In 1950 the residential and commercial sector consumed almost a quarter of the total; by 1980 less than 1% of coal went to those sectors. In transportation, steam locomotives (and some coal-fired marine transportation) consumed 13% of coal; by 1970 they were all replaced with diesel-burning or electric engines. Industry consumed 46% of coal in 1950; by 2000 less than 10% of coal was consumed by that sector. Meanwhile, the electric power sector, which consumed less than 20% of the half-billion tons of coal burned in 1950, used more than 90% of the billion-plus tons consumed in 2011.

Table 8. Coal Consumption by Sector, 1950-2010

	Total Consumption (million tons)	Percent Consumed by Sector			
		Residential-Commercial	Industrial	Transportation	Electric
1950	494.1	23.2%	45.5%	12.8%	18.6%
1955	447.0	15.3%	48.7%	3.8%	32.2%
1960	398.1	10.3%	44.6%	0.8%	44.4%
1965	472.0	5.4%	42.6%	0.1%	51.9%
1970	523.2	3.1%	35.7%	0.1%	61.2%
1975	562.6	1.7%	26.2%	–	72.2%
1980	702.7	0.9%	18.1%	–	81.0%
1985	818.0	1.0%	14.2%	–	84.8%
1990	904.5	0.7%	12.7%	–	86.5%
1995	962.1	0.6%	11.0%	–	88.4%
2000	1,084.1	0.4%	8.7%	–	90.9%
2005	1,126.0	0.4%	7.4%	–	92.1%
2006	1,112.3	0.3%	7.4%	–	92.3%
2007	1,128.0	0.3%	7.0%	–	92.7%
2008	1,120.5	0.3%	6.8%	–	92.9%
2009	997.5	0.3%	6.1%	–	93.6%
2010P	1,048.3	0.3%	6.6%	–	93.1%

Source: EIA, *Annual Energy Review 2010*, Table 7.3.

Notes: Data for 2010 are preliminary.

Renewables

The major supply of renewable energy in the United States, not counting hydroelectric power generation, is fuel ethanol. Consumption in the United States in 2011 was about 14.0 billion gallons, mainly blended into E10 gasohol (a blend of 10% ethanol and 90% gasoline). This figure represents 10.2% of the approximately 136 billion gallons of gasoline consumption in the same year. As **Figure 19** indicates, fuel ethanol production has increased rapidly in recent years, especially since the phasing out of the fuel additive methyl tertiary butyl ether (MTBE), and the establishment of the renewable fuel standard (RFS) which requires the use of biofuels in transportation.

Figure 19. U.S. Ethanol Production, 1990-2011

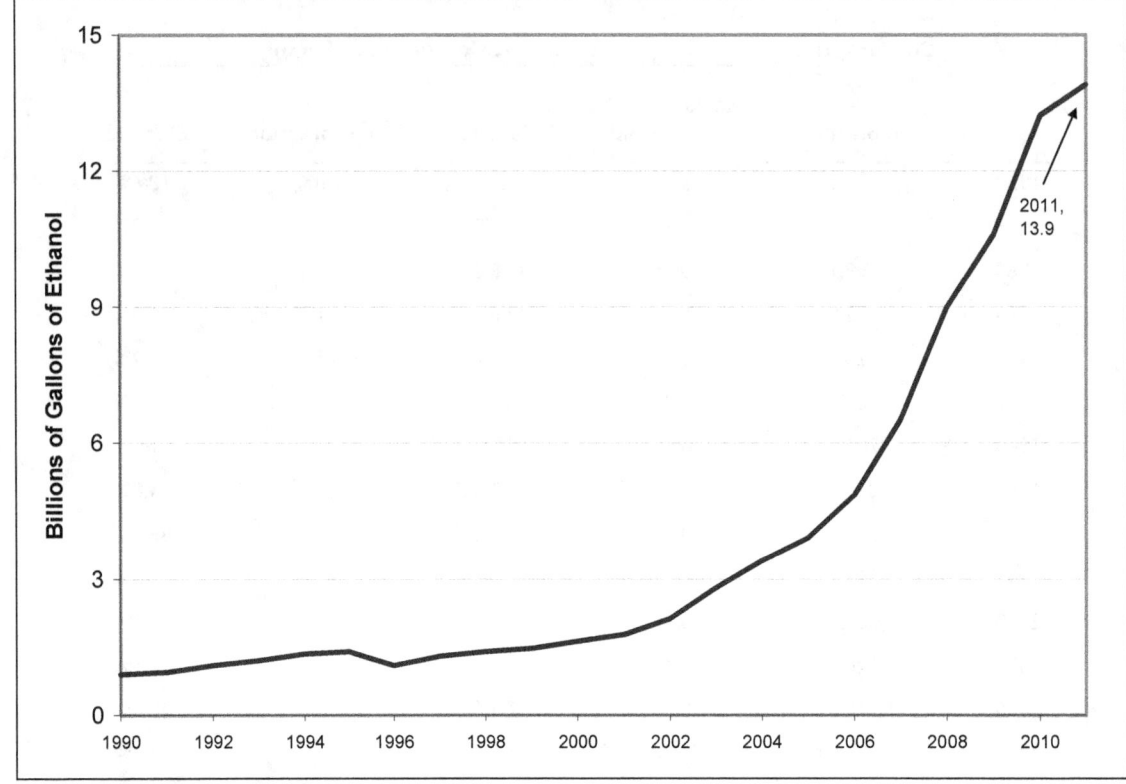

Source: Renewable Fuels Association, March 13, 2012. http://www.ethanolrfa.org/pages/statistics/.

Another rapidly growing renewable resource is wind-generated electric power, as shown in **Figure 20**. The 120 billion kwh of wind energy produced in 2011 is about 3% of the 4,100 billion kwh of total electricity generation in that year.

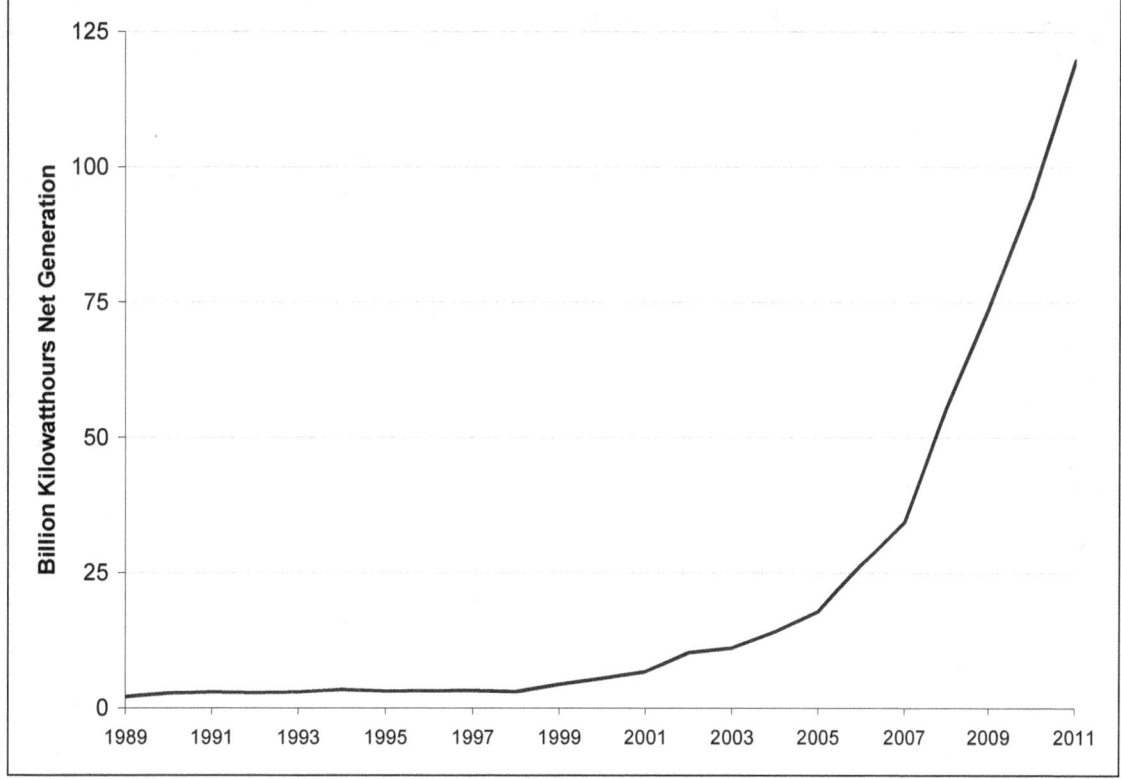

Figure 20. Wind Electricity Net Generation, 1989-2011

Source: EIA, *Monthly Energy Review*, March 2012, Table 7.2a.

Notes: Data are for electric utilities, independent power producers, commercial plants, and industrial plants.

Conservation and Energy Efficiency

Vehicle Fuel Economy

Energy efficiency has been a popular goal of policy makers in responding to the repeated energy crises of recent decades, and efforts to reduce the energy intensity of a broad spectrum of economic activities have been made both at the government and private level. Because of the transportation sector's near total dependence on vulnerable oil supplies, improving the efficiency of motor vehicles has been of particular interest. (For an analysis of legislative policies to improve vehicle fuel economy, see CRS Report R40166, *Automobile and Light Truck Fuel Economy: The CAFE Standards*, by Brent D. Yacobucci.) **Figure 21** illustrates the trends in this effort for passenger cars and for light trucks, vans, and sport utility vehicles.

Figure 21. Light Duty Vehicle Fuel Efficiency Rates, 1973-2011

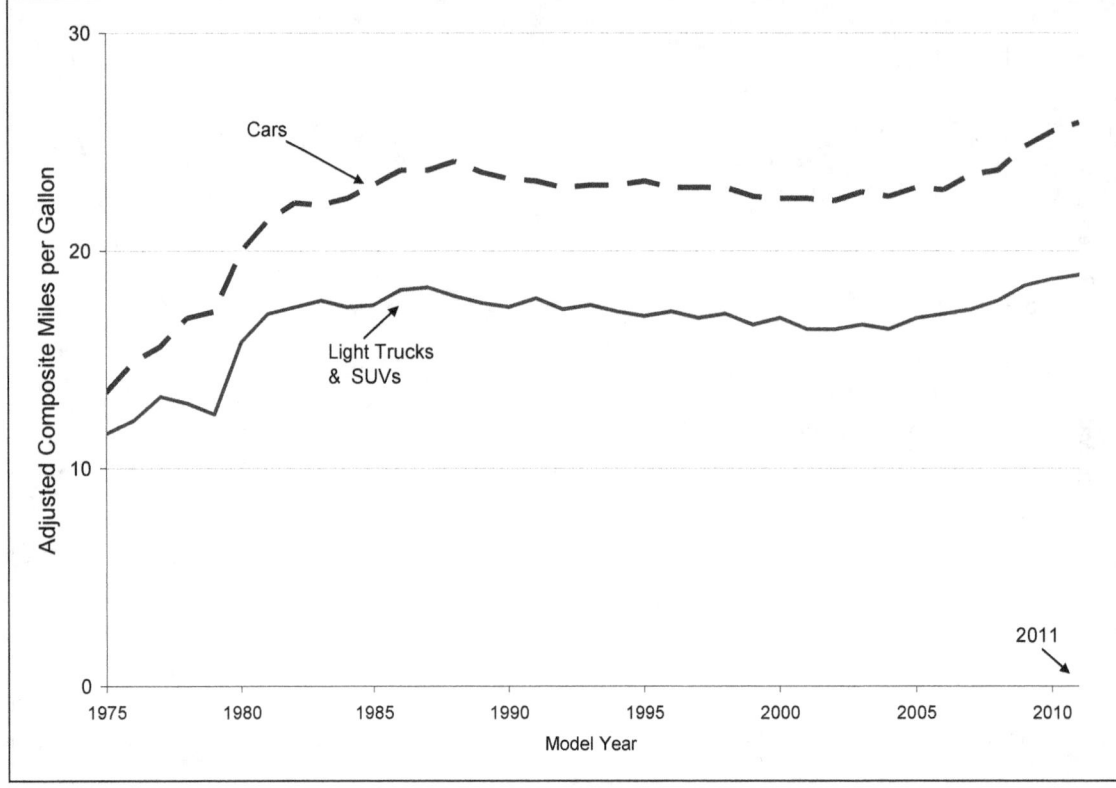

Source: Environmental Protection Agency. Light-Duty Automotive Technology, Carbon Dioxide Emissions, and Fuel Economy Trends: 1975 Through 2011. Table 1. March 2012. http://www.epa.gov/otaq/fetrends.htm.

Analysis by the Environmental Protection Agency (EPA),[7] involving the composition of the fleet as well as the per-vehicle fuel rates, indicates that light vehicle fuel economy declined on average between 1988 and 2003. This is largely because of increased weight, higher performance, and a higher proportion of sport utility vehicles and light trucks sold. In 2003, SUVs, pickups, and vans comprised 48% of all sales, more than twice their market share in 1983. After 2004 fuel economy improved and the market share of trucks declined. Further, tighter fuel economy standards for light trucks were implemented beginning in model year 2005.

Energy Consumption and GDP

A frequent point of concern in formulating energy policy is the relationship between economic growth and energy use. It seems obvious that greater economic activity would bring with it increased energy consumption, although many other factors affecting consumption make the short-term relationship highly variable. Over a longer period, for some energy-related activities, the relationship with economic growth has been essentially level. For the period from 1973 to 2010, for instance, consumption of electricity remained close to 0.4 kwh per constant dollar of GDP.

---

[7] U.S. EPA, Light-Duty Automotive Technology, Carbon Dioxide Emissions, and Fuel Economy Trends: 1975 Through 2011, March, 2012. http://www.epa.gov/otaq/fetrends.htm

In the case of oil and gas, however, a remarkable drop took place in the ratio of consumption to economic growth following the price spikes and supply disruptions of the 1970s, as illustrated in **Figure 22**. Consumption of oil and gas declined from 14,000 Btus per constant dollar of GDP in 1973 to a little more than 8,000 in 1985, and has continued to decline at a slower rate since then.

Figure 22. Oil and Natural Gas Consumption per Dollar of GDP, 1973-2010

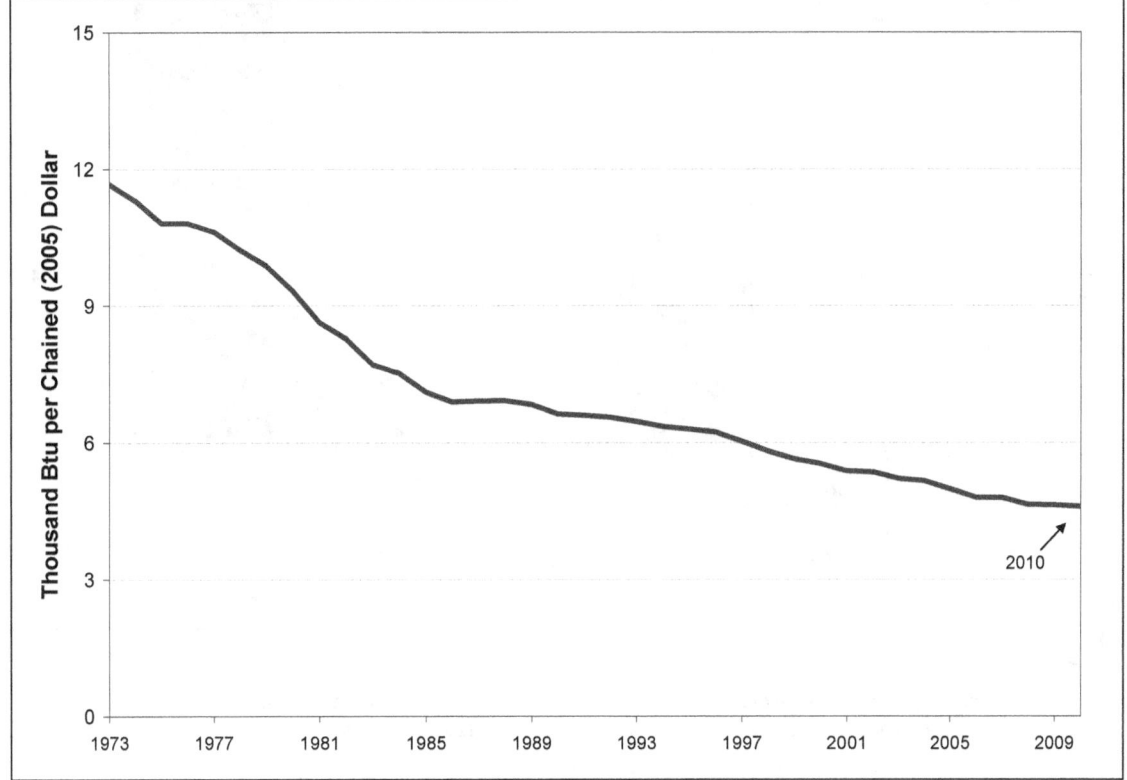

Source: EIA, *Monthly Energy Review*, February 2012, Table 1.7.

During the earlier period, oil and gas consumption actually declined 15% while GDP, despite many economic problems with inflation and slow growth, was increasing by 44% (see **Figure 23**). During the period 1987 to 2010, oil and gas consumption increased by about 20%, while GDP increased 79%.

Figure 23. Change in Oil and Natural Gas Consumption and Growth in GDP, 1973-2010

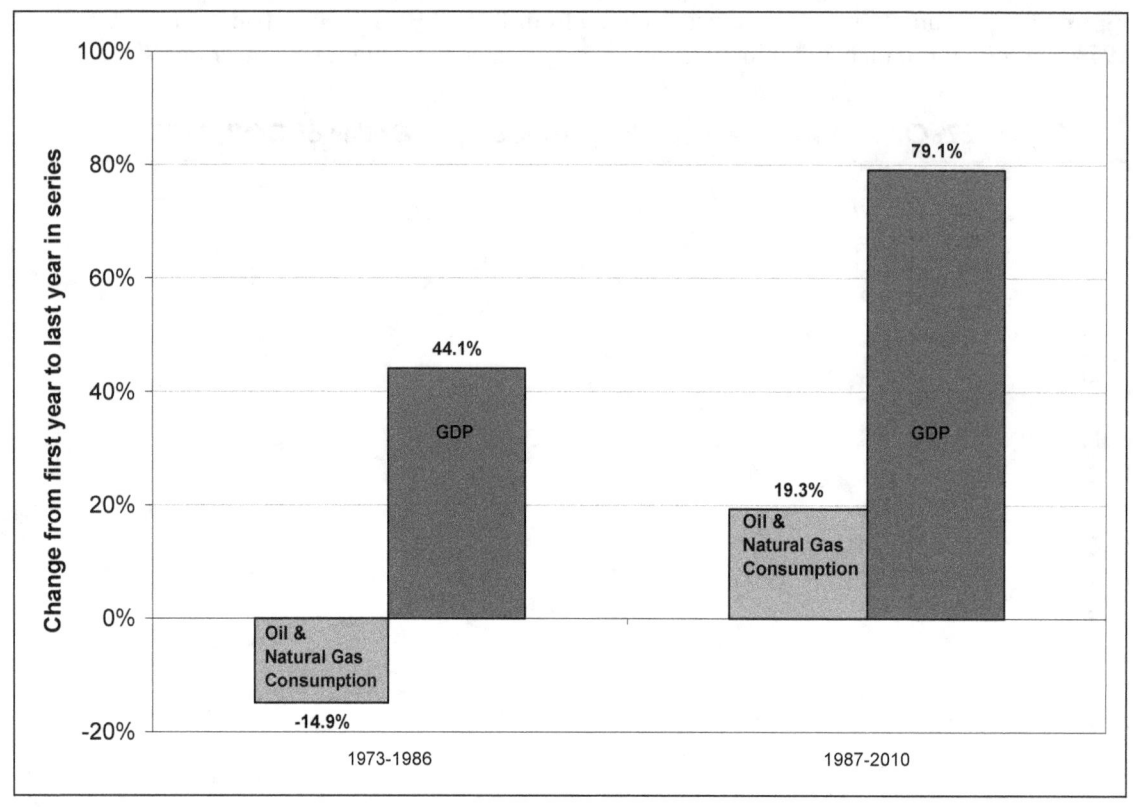

Source: EIA, *Monthly Energy Review*, February 2012, Table 1.7.

Notes: Percentages calculated by CRS. Percent change in oil and natural gas consumption measured in quadrillion Btu. Percent change in GDP based on billion chained (2005) dollars.

Major Statistical Resources

Energy Information Administration (EIA)

EIA home page—http://www.eia.doe.gov

Most of the tables and figures in this report are derived from databases maintained by the Energy Information Administration (EIA), an independent agency of the Department of Energy. EIA's Website presents the complete text of its many statistical reports in PDF's and Excel files.

EIA, Publications and Reports—http://www.eia.doe.gov/bookshelf.html

EIA's most frequently requested reports include the following:

Annual Energy Review: all the historical yearly energy data across fuels

Annual Energy Outlook: energy projections out to 2035

Country Analysis Briefs: country-level energy overviews

Electric Power Monthly: monthly summary of electric power generation and capacity

International Energy Annual: international historical yearly energy data across fuels

International Energy Outlook: worldwide energy projections to 2025

Monthly Energy Review: all the latest monthly energy data across fuels

This Week in Petroleum: weekly prices and analytical summary of the petroleum industry

Weekly Petroleum Status Report: weekly petroleum prices, production and stocks data

Other Sources

Nuclear Regulatory Commission Information Digest: http://www.nrc.gov/reading-rm/doc-collections/nuregs/staff/sr1350/

Updated annually, this official NRC publication (NUREG-1350) includes general statistics on U.S. and worldwide nuclear power production, U.S. nuclear reactors, and radioactive waste

American Petroleum Institute (API): http://api-ec.api.org/newsplashpage/index.cfm

The primary trade association of the oil and natural gas industry representing more than 400 members. Research, programs, and publications on public policy, technical standards, industry statistics, and regulations.

API: State Gasoline Tax Reports: http://www.api.org/statistics/fueltaxes/index.cfm

Bloomberg.Com, Market Data: Commodities, Energy Prices: http://www.bloomberg.com/energy/index.html

Displays four tables:

- Petroleum ($/bbl) for crude oil. The generally accepted price for crude oil is "WTI Cushing $" which is listed third in the table.

- Petroleum (¢/gal) for heating oil and gasoline.

- Natural Gas ($/MMBtu)

- Electricity ($/megawatt hour)

This site is updated two to three times per day.

AAA's Daily Fuel Gauge Report: http://www.fuelgaugereport.com/index.asp

At-the-pump retail fuel prices for gasoline and diesel fuel. Gives average price for today, yesterday, a month ago and a year ago for wholesale and crude oil. Also displays line chart showing the averages for the previous 12 months. National, state, and metropolitan data.

International Energy Agency: http://www.iea.org

The International Energy Agency is an autonomous body within the Organization for Economic Co-operation and Development (OECD). It gathers and analyzes statistics and "disseminates information on the world energy market and seeks to promote stable international trade in energy."

A subscription is required to access most of the information on this website, although a limited amount of information is available to nonsubscribers. Members of Congress and their staff should contact CRS for a copy of anything that requires a subscription.

Author Contact Information

Carl E. Behrens
Specialist in Energy Policy
cbehrens@crs.loc.gov, 7-8303

Carol Glover
Information Research Specialist
cglover@crs.loc.gov, 7-7353

Key Policy Staff

Area of Expertise	Name	Phone	E-mail
Introduction and General	Carl Behrens	7-8303	cbehrens@crs.loc.gov
Oil	Robert Pirog	7-6847	rpirog@crs.loc.gov
	Neelesh Nerurkar	7-2873	nnerurkar@crs.loc.gov
Energy Taxes	Robert Pirog	7-6847	rpirog@crs.loc.gov
Electricity	Richard Campbell	7-7905	rcampbell@crs.loc.gov
Natural Gas	Robert Pirog	7-6847	rpirog@crs.loc.gov
	Michael Ratner	7-9529	mratner@crs.loc.gov
Coal	Anthony Andrews	7-6843	aandrews@crs.loc.gov
Nuclear Energy	Mark Holt	7-1704	mholt@crs.loc.gov
Conservation, Energy Efficiency, and Renewable Energy	Fred Sissine	7-7039	fsissine@crs.loc.gov
CAFE Standards (vehicle fuel economy)	Brent Yacobucci	7-9662	byacobucci@crs.loc.gov
Statistics, Tables, Figures	Carol Glover	7-7353	cglover@crs.loc.gov